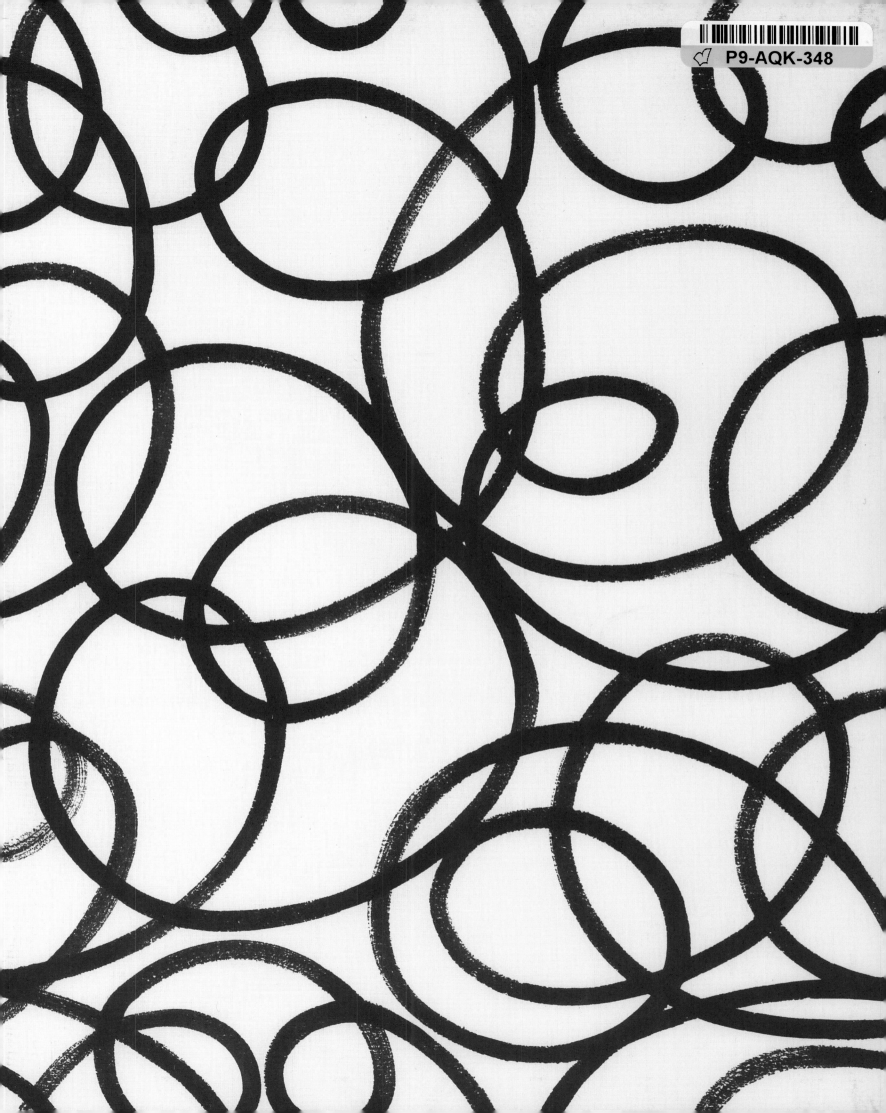

To my friend Bill
All my love

Dedicated to Robin Roberts
for his vision, creativity, and kindness

Karim

CLARENCE HOUSE

THE ART OF THE TEXTILE FABRIC FOR THE INSPIRED HOME

KAZUMI YOSHIDA

with Sabine Rothman

Photography by François Halard   Styling by Noemi Bonazzi

RIZZOLI
NEW YORK

New York · Paris · London · Milan

Table of Contents

Foreword

Kazumi's work strives for the universal.

His take on nature is vivid, focused, and inspired. Art that is captivating, poetic, and free.

His oeuvre is deeply rooted in the twentieth century: that of Matisse and Basquiat, via Picasso and Cocteau, which continues to thrill us, and will do for generations to come.

I was lucky enough to be introduced to Kazumi's work during my first foray into the workplace in the world of textiles at Ratti. Kazumi's designs for Clarence House were then the epitome of refinement and the benchmark for quality upholstery. I was well schooled—my eye for design was honed and it signaled the path I was to take. Much like Morandi, Kazumi studies the very essence of things.

He re-creates the natural world with elegance, fantasy, and a certain levity, in the perpetual quest for the endless beauty of life. **PIERRE-ALEXIS DUMAS** CHIEF CREATIVE OFFICER, HERMÈS INTERNATIONAL

Page 4: Japanese photographer Koji Yano interpreted the energy of Clarence House in an image that marries a scarf flung into the air with a vivid fluorescent background. Opposite: *Hommage à Cocteau*, a silk-and-linen brocatelle, is an adaptation of a French Renaissance fabric from the archives of Bucol, a mill owned by Hermès. Stylized sunbursts and flames inspired by the Jean Cocteau film *La Belle et la Bête* were substituted for the original fabric's lilies.

Foreword

I've been following Kazumi Yoshida's work with great interest and indeed passion since the early 1980s, when he first started working with Robin Roberts and became the creative director at Clarence House.

This partnership led to America's acquainting itself with new tastes and new aesthetic benchmarks through the spread of fine fabrics from Europe never seen until then. The result has seen Clarence House becoming the present-day symbol and style-setter for the world of interior design.

Kazumi has thus brought about an important creative revolution by introducing a new, quintessentially Japanese brand of aesthetics, along with a new way of conceiving beauty. Sophisticated, modern, visualized research that juxtaposes "emptiness" with the "fullness" of Western culture, the sense of incompleteness, and the asymmetrical; the result is the very height of evocativeness, whereby a decoration with a clear-cut sign represents insight into an aspect of reality, although it can never be completely grasped.

Kazumi has shown us the way toward essentiality, gradually reducing figuration to the bare bones. In doing so he has taken us in the direction of Japanese aestheticism of the "aware," the emotive quality innate in nature, in art, and in the emotional reaction of a person faced with aesthetic expression, the emotion of things and the beautiful fleetingness of the world.

He has found an innovative way to combine Japanese tradition with American culture to perfection. In doing so he has found new dynamics, resulting in a new and eclectic taste that introduces an exotic feel in the world of fabrics. Color becomes crucial in its Japanese connotation between ethnic and aesthetic, in the refined combinations of color and the pairing of hues that attain the highest form of expression.

The distinctiveness, the actual potential in the refined aesthetic sensitivity of Kazumi Yoshida, resides in something very subtle indeed.

JACOPO ETRO CREATIVE DIRECTOR OF TEXTILES, ACCESSORIES, AND HOME DEPARTMENT, ETRO

Opposite: *Flowering Quince*, one of Clarence House's most beloved designs, embodies a fascination with nature and the marriage of East and West, which are evident in some of Kazumi Yoshida's most compelling work. Using techniques from Japanese brush painting, the pattern combines speed, lightness, and fluidity—the hallmarks of Kazumi's gestural signature—with a staccato rhythm and pretty, abstract blossoms. Everything contributes to a remarkable sense of balance.

Introduction

Clarence House was founded by Robin Roberts fifty years ago, a time when the design community was under the dominant influence of English designers as well as English furniture and fabric design. There was little influence—and almost no products—coming from the Continent. It was this void that Robin sought to fill during his many trips to Paris and in his subsequent decision to start Clarence House.

The founding ideology of Clarence House, which always guided Robin in his selection of products for the company, was that all good design must adhere to a strict coda of design rules. These principles pertained to all aspects of design: fabrics, furniture, and even the design process itself. These principles were not so much universal aesthetic tenets that we might ascribe to discussions of art or music. Rather, they were historical and archival principles, embedded in the evolution of design and with which Robin was intimately familiar—principles that he subscribed to as the formula for the growth of Clarence House.

In addition to archival products, Robin was able to attract the best collections available in Europe, firms that wanted to have their products displayed in the showrooms of Clarence House, which was fast becoming the destination of choice for smart and sophisticated designers throughout America. Manuel Canovas, Etro, Osborne & Little, Colefax and Fowler, all called Clarence House home and all benefited from the growth of the company and the brilliant showmanship of Robin Roberts. While each of these lines took certain liberties in their design direction, they were still essentially a reverberation of the baroque, archival style of Robin Roberts, albeit perhaps in a stylized version of his point of view.

In the late seventies, Clarence House held sway over the design community, and Robin Roberts had established himself as a larger-than-life figure in the interior-design world. One thing was missing, however, and Kazumi

Opposite: A detail of the sculpture above the fireplace in Kazumi Yoshida's New York apartment with a swatch of *Rayure Satin Monceau*, a striped satin fabric, tucked into it.

Introduction

Yoshida fulfilled that need. The missing piece for Clarence House was an in-house signature, a design statement that truly set the company apart from the staid, traditional, documentary world that we accepted as the paradigm for the world of high-end design.

The arrival of Kazumi brought a new energy and new influences—an inherent aesthetic that began Clarence House's move away from the archival influences and into the stylized worlds of art and fashion. Kazumi was being educated by Robin in the historical waves of design founded mostly on the Continent, and he was interpreting these movements through his unique eye (and hand), filtering them through his knowledge of the great artists and fashion designers that he so admired.

The team of Robin and Kazumi established a new benchmark for creativity in both prints and wovens, yet Clarence House was still "Robin's" Clarence House and the product, while stylized and artistic to a point, was still what I would refer to as "period faithful." Kazumi, out of respect and admiration for Robin and perhaps because he relied so much on him for direction and vision, restrained his artistic exuberance. While there was frivolity and glamour, there was still not the completely free artistic expression that was to come later—and which is evident in this book.

After 9/11 there were major events that altered the direction of Clarence House. Business suffered dramatically as did Robin's health. Robin asked Peter Kaufmann, an old friend and colleague, to come in and rescue the company, which Peter was happy to do. Clarence House is today the crown jewel in the corporate stable of P/Kaufmann Inc.

The most difficult element in the transition was that Kazumi, the resident artist, had lost his muse. There was no longer anyone to define the parameters and limits to which Kazumi's creative efforts must adhere. The company could no longer survive as "Robin's" Clarence House, because Robin was no longer around. The only hope for the firm was that it could be transformed into "Kazumi's" Clarence House—free from archival restraint, youthful, energetic, and artistic in the fullest and freest sense. The new Clarence House is not a stylized version of a historical document but new artwork itself. As you can see in this book, Clarence House has evolved. From Robin, to Robin and Kazumi, to Kazumi, the product has developed but the bar has never been lowered. The history of Clarence House is a history of glamour, luxury, and art served to the world by two extraordinarily talented people. **ROBERT APPELBAUM** PRESIDENT, CLARENCE HOUSE

Opposite: A study of the silk cut velvet pattern *Labyrinth*. A sterling example of timeless elegance, it would look completely at home in a modern interior but nods to ancient motifs. Gathered at top left, a swatch of *Zèbre Velours Soie* (Zebra Silk Velvet), a fabric that renders the sure appeal of animal patterns in the most luxurious material.

Clarence House: Looking Back

December 18, 2007. Property from the estate of Robin Roberts is being auctioned at Christie's. The star of the show is a bronze armchair designed by the great Art Deco designer Armand-Albert Rateau around 1920—one of six that collectors George and Florence Blumenthal commissioned for the pool in their Manhattan town house. Going once. Going twice. Sold—for $2,001,000. It's no wonder Robin was attracted to this piece, once owned by such a grand couple. (He was head of Lazard Frères and a former president of the Metropolitan Museum of Art; she was aunt to Katharine Graham.) As founder of Clarence House, the nonpareil of American textile firms, Robin could never resist a thing of beauty. Rateau had crossed classical antiquity with aquatic motifs and created a chair that was refined and elegant, yet avant-garde for its time. The value of extraordinary artistry such as this mattered to Robin, much more than cost. But provenance always was a draw for him.

It's a bit ironic actually, for Robin Roberts's own provenance was a bit less lofty than it might have appeared to someone who met him later in life. But that's why he understood the cachet of a storied past, the luxury of a legacy—he had invented his own and that of his company, Clarence House. He was a self-made man.

Robin Roberts's life story is a remarkable tale of self-invention. Born as Robert Bernard Schwaid in 1929, he was the third son of a New York dentist, respectably middle class. He grew up on Long Island and the Upper West Side. After dropping out of the University of Wisconsin, he got a job as a dancing teacher at the Fred Astaire Dance Studios in New York City. (His nickname was Rumba, after his particular specialty.) The consummate salesman, he sold courses like crazy—and was madly successful. And why not? He had good looks and plenty of chutzpah. But even then, he had an eye for luxury—and was living somewhat beyond his means. That penchant for excess was the seed from which Clarence House grew.

If not for a classified ad in the *New York Times*, there might be no Clarence House. Robin was stretched thin and couldn't quite afford his apartment. So he advertised for a roommate. As it happened, the first person to respond was the (then) up-and-coming interior designer Keith Irvine. Keith had been trained at Colefax and Fowler in

Opposite: Home to Clarence House in its early years, the former Murphy town house at 40 East 57th Street was a glorious expression of Robin's aspirations for his brand— exclusive, pedigreed, incredibly chic, and full of life. On one of Manhattan's toniest shopping stretches, the building boasted storefront windows that were the talk of the town.

Clarence House: Looking Back

London and had come to the States to work with Sister Parish on a Georgetown town house for Senator John F. Kennedy, the future president. Keith recalls walking into Robin's apartment, where he found a refrigerator stocked with nothing but Champagne and caviar. Needless to say, he moved in.

It was about this time that Robert Schwaid became Robin Roberts. Changing his name was just the first step toward a complete re-creation of himself as a grand character, an aesthetic impresario. Why did he choose Robin Roberts? It was the name of a famous baseball player. He thought it would seem vaguely familiar to anyone who heard it—and therefore memorable. But who in his milieu followed baseball? He could be pretty sure no one would ever question him.

Inspired by Irvine, Robin started taking classes at the New York School of Interior Design and got a job as an assistant in a decorating firm, from which he was soon fired for cheekily answering the phone, "Roberts & Irvine." But he was as prescient as he was audacious. Shortly, the pair did team up. They started decorating together as Roberts & Irvine for elite clients such as Mr. and Mrs. Averell Harriman. Ever the showmen, Robin and Keith hired the best public relations firm in town to create a stir. The duo had almost no cash, but left an entirely different impression. And eventually, the impression became more and more the reality.

Robin and Keith were importing fabrics from Europe to use in their decorating projects—embossed velvets, traditional floral chintz, chinoiserie florals, eighteenth- and nineteenth-century-style damasks and jacquards.

Opposite: Kazumi's three-dimensional artwork depicting the famous patinated bronze Armand-Albert Rateau chair that was the star of Robin's personal collection. *Armand*, a silk cut velvet based on the chair's fish motif, is a recent addition to the line. Its opulence recalls the days of grand luxe; its modernity suits Clarence House now, as then.

EUROPE'S FINEST FABRICS

CLARENCE HOUSE*

We take great pride in announcing the opening of our first showroom in the United States, bringing to the American designer the finest decorative fabrics available in Europe.

38 EAST 57 STREET, NEW YORK   PLAZA 2-2890

*Clarence House is the London residence of Her Majesty Queen Elizabeth, The Queen Mother.

Clarence House: Looking Back

As their work became known, other designers expressed interest in their fabric sources. Robin could see there was clearly a market for the variety of textiles that he and Keith were after. He promptly borrowed $10,000 from his father so that they could start a fabric business on the side.

At the time Brunschwig & Fils, which had started in France as a tapestry-weaving mill and opened operations in the United States in 1925, was one of the few companies importing cloth from England and France. The firm had distribution deals with most of the European mills that Robin set out to work with. (Despite the European-sounding name, Scalamandré had been manufacturing silks in the United States since the 1920s. And Old World Weavers, which Iris and Carl Apfel started in 1950, specialized in weaving exact reproductions of antique fabrics.) But Robin saw an opportunity. He went to Europe and negotiated with the mills to break their exclusivity with Brunschwig and work with him as well. He came back to New York with samples—primarily eighteenth-century brocades and damasks from a potpourri of French houses, including Lelièvre, Tassinari & Chatel, Prelle, Le Manach, and Charles Burger. In 1961, he and Keith opened a small showroom at 38 East 57th Street. Clarence House was born.

Robin started with typical ceremony, running an advertisement that heralded the opening of Clarence House's first showroom in the United States. Of course, it was his and Keith's only showroom, but it sounded as if they had a venerable history. They had about twenty hanging wings of fabric—and a lot of hoopla.

How did they decide to call their new venture Clarence House? When Keith and Robin were in the planning stage, the Queen Mother, who was living at the royal residence Clarence House, had announced Princess Margaret's engagement to Antony Armstrong-Jones. So the name was in the air. Robin thought it sounded both established and impressive, yet it was vague enough not to get them in trouble. "We couldn't call it Buckingham Palace," he sometimes remarked. The name was meant to set the tone. It was meant to exude grandeur, luxury, and a sense of heritage. And it did. Reportedly, one of Robin's somewhat snooty customers, an uptown society lady, told him

Opposite: The original announcement for the grand opening of Clarence House textiles did everything to suggest a relationship with the British royal family without actually claiming one. Typically brash, it heralded the arrival of Clarence House's first American showroom—without indicating that this was in fact the company's only showroom.

Clarence House: Looking Back

early on that she was so happy he had opened in New York because she always shopped at Clarence House in London. It was typical of Robin to have a little fun with people, playing to their pretensions as he honed his own. With typical tongue-in-cheek humor, Robin and Keith kept a picture of the Queen Mother prominently displayed upstairs in the showroom. And if people did ask what the connection to the original Clarence House was, Robin would brush it off, shutting down the inquiry with this standard clever retort: "We are not at liberty to say."

After less than a year, Robin and Keith went in different directions. Keith stayed focused on decorating while Robin took over the fabric business. Some years later, the enterprise moved a few doors down to the elegant Murphy town house at 40 East 57th Street. The grandeur of this landmark nineteenth-century building suited the Clarence House image that Robin was trying to nurture. Roslyn Rosier, a highly influential dealer-decorator and one of interior designer Albert Hadley's first bosses, had occupied the space for many years. When Robin heard she had died, he ran right over and secured the space, which was to be the firm's home for many years. Despite his taste for glamour, Robin always counseled appropriateness, and the offerings did range from simple cotton canvas to extravagant hand-loomed brocades. He introduced Americans to fabrics from Colefax and Fowler, Liberty, Pierre Frey, Manuel Canovas, Osborne & Little, Lelièvre, and so many more. There was plenty to choose from, some fabric the finest in the world, some more accessible.

Almost everyone describes walking into Clarence House for the first time as an intimidating experience. The receptionists were very strict—everyone had to show credentials, even Greta Garbo, who signed in using the name Mrs. Brown. (She wasn't the only star who wandered in. Despite his strict decorators-only policy, Robin loved

Opposite: At the beginning, Clarence House imported European fabrics, like this architectonic silk cut velvet, *Velours Quadrille*, from the Quenin mill's archives. It bears the firm's original label, which is emblazoned with an image of the British royal residence. This particular fabric, shown in two colorways, was a favorite of the late style-setter Tina Chow.

celebrities and they were always welcome: Gloria Swanson, Ethel Merman, Claudette Colbert, Paloma Picasso, Tina Chow, Diana Ross, and Lee Radziwill to name a few.) Every decorator worth his or her salt shopped there: Billy Baldwin, Jed Johnson, Sister Parish, Albert Hadley, and Mark Hampton. It felt like a private club at times—fabulous people just hanging out, socializing as much as working—in extraordinary surroundings.

The double-height reception area was elegantly kitted out with antique furniture covered in traditional fabrics, modern sculpture, and whitewashed Pecky cypress paneling. Using that rustic wood to tone down the opulence was genius—a signal that this place wasn't about period rooms, but living well in the here and now. A grand staircase led up to the showroom spaces, filled with racks of hanging fabric on the mezzanine and on the third floor, which was the former ballroom and still had its beautiful floors and fluted Corinthian columns. The building's bowfront third-floor facade of French doors and a window—it still exists—overlooked 57th Street. At Christmastime, Robin would have trumpeters playing carols from the balcony with the windows open. The showroom was freezing, but what's a little suffering for pomp and circumstance? Period textiles from the company's archives were framed and displayed as artworks, hung salon-style in the stairwell. A well-appointed salon, designed for the presentation of woven fabrics, had walls and furniture upholstered in plain and embossed taupe linen velvet. The whimsical trimmings salon sported antique antlers festooned with colorful tiebacks. And a little elevator was upholstered in tufted caramel suede. Offices on the fourth floor eventually included the design studio, brought in-house in the mid-1970s so that Clarence House could produce some of its own original designs. In addition to the New York showroom, Robin set up a distribution network across America. Early on, he got particular help from Dorothy Kneedler Lawenda and Harry Lawenda, the owners of Kneedler-Fauchere, a home-furnishings distributor that had started in post–World War II San Francisco and expanded to showrooms in Los Angeles and Denver.

Opposite, top: The display windows at the 57th Street mansion were often outrageous—here, barbed wire and a skeleton paired with *Mongolia*, a printed cotton. Opposite, below: Painter and textile designer Sonia Delaunay inspired this 1984 window display by Robert Currie featuring *Gropius*, a cut-and-uncut linen from a document in the Fadini-Borghi archives. Proceeding spread: For a holiday window, Robert Currie imagined three wise women, dressed by fashion designer Norma Kamali, on their way to Bethlehem.

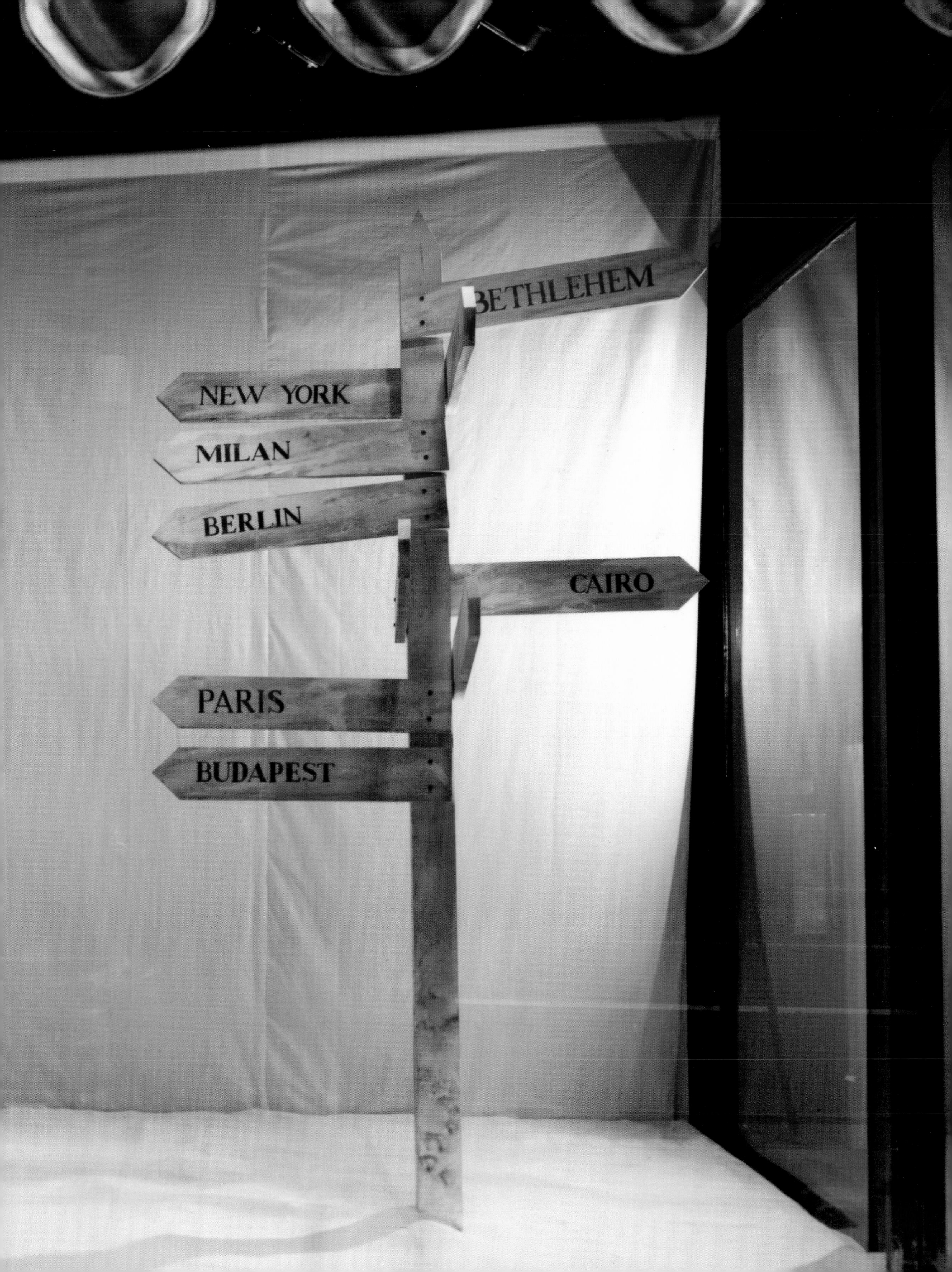
BETHLEHEM
NEW YORK
MILAN
BERLIN
CAIRO
PARIS
BUDAPEST

Clarence House: Looking Back

The Lawendas famously pioneered the idea of the multiline showroom representing many different designers and manufacturers. Soon after Robin and Keith opened Clarence House, the Lawendas read an article in a trade newspaper about the launch. At the time, the couple were looking for a strong collection of textiles, so they gave Robin a call. He flew out to meet them with a small suitcase of fabrics, which they liked very much. Because Robin couldn't afford to have the necessary samples created to sell the line, the Lawendas floated him the money to bring Clarence House to the California market.

The town house was the stage on which Robin's flair for the dramatic unfolded. But it was also his place to play—and sometimes to shock the establishment. Robin saw the town house's windows as more than a mere storefront. The displays were a showcase for Clarence House's creativity. They were meant to provoke, surprise, amaze, and delight. He designed some of the most outrageous ones himself. But from 1965 to 1973, Robin hired Gene Moore, the creative director who was simultaneously working on Tiffany & Co.'s brilliant window vignettes, which he masterminded until 1995. At Clarence House, Moore advanced Robin's avant-garde aspirations with installations such as one in which he paired Clarence House fabrics with a motorcycle, whips, and chains. And when he moved on, Robin turned to Robert Currie, a display artist and set designer who eventually turned decorator himself. In Bob's hands, the Clarence House windows reached new heights as a form of experimental street theater. The scenarios were outrageous at times—one an ersatz beauty parlor, another a psychiatrist's office. He arranged barbed wire around a Persian carpet scattered with "human" bones. A life-size gorilla was buried under a huge pile of bananas. A gigantic caterpillar drawn from *Alice in Wonderland*—but with Robin's face—lounged amid luxurious fabrics. One Christmas, three wise women in Norma Kamali outifts stopped in the Clarence House window on their way to Bethlehem, inviting a scolding from the archdiocese. And so on. Robin's budget was seemingly limitless—perhaps $20,000 for every window change, six times a year. "Whatever it takes," he used to say.

Opposite: When Clarence House moved from the town house to the D&D Building at 211 East 58th Street, the windows were no less lavish than they had been. Here, rabbits frolic in a circus atmosphere with *Toile La Fontaine* as their background—a whimsical toile de Jouy brought to life. Proceeding spread: Clarence House's classic advertisements from the 1980s and 1990s were striking in their graphic simplicity—half a sofa clad in a signature fabric, against a solid background; left: *Matisse*; right: clockwise from top left: *Gropius, Poissonnière, Jeu de Cartes,* and *La Jungle.*

clarence house

clarence house

211 EAST 58 STREET   NEW YORK   THROUGH DECORATORS AND ARCHITECTS

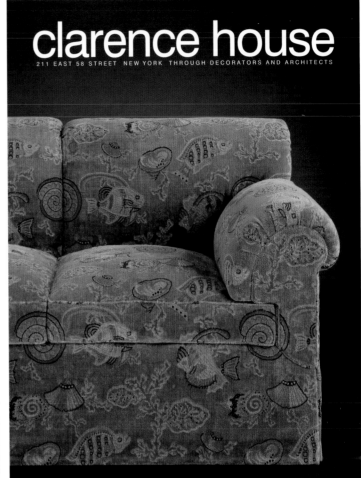

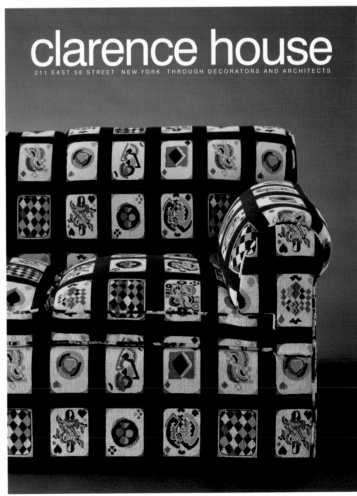

CLARENCEHOUSE

IS PROUD TO LAUNCH OUR FIRST OUTDOOR COLLECTION.

CLARENCEHOUSE

Through Decorators and Architects • Fabric, Trimmings, Wallcoverings
800 803-2850

CLARENCEHOUSE

Through Decorators and Architects • Fabric, Trimmings, Wallcoverings
212-292-3440 • www.clarencehouse.com
Turnell & Gigon Group, Chelsea Harbour Design Centre, London SW10 0XE
44(0)20 7259 7280 • www.tandggroup.com

CLARENCEHOUSE

Through Decorators and Architects • Fabric, Trimmings, Wallcoverings • 800 803-2850

CLARENCE HOUSE

CLARENCE HOUSE

Clarence House: Looking Back

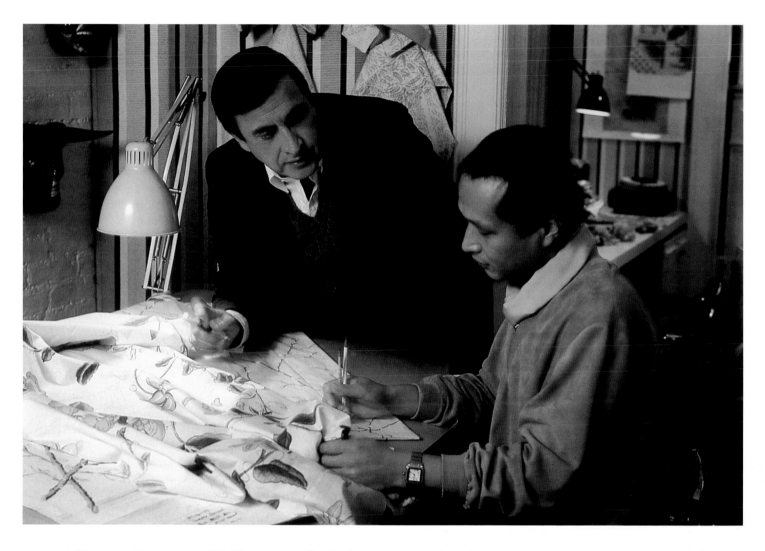

I joined Clarence House in 1981. The reason Robin hired me was that Clarence House was on the cusp of change. The company had licensing and royalty deals to fulfill with Bernardaud Limoges for china, Cannon Mills for bedding, Imperial for wall coverings, and P/Kaufmann for fabric. (Robin's close working relationship with Peter Kaufmann was one of the reasons that the latter's company, P/Kaufmann Inc., got the nod when Robin decided to sell Clarence House in 2002.) Plus the firm needed new fabrics of its own because companies like Manuel Canovas and Osborne & Little were finally able to open their own operations in the United States and didn't need Clarence House as a distributor any longer. When the European companies decamped, it seriously reduced the number of designs we were able to offer. Robin was working with freelancers and had a bare-bones design studio that was not equipped to meet the new demands. He didn't have anyone who could execute his ideas.

My audition was a freelance assignment. And I proved myself with my first design—*Papiers Japonais*. It's still a Clarence House classic. This trompe l'oeil design depicts delicate botanical sketches on pieces of antique rice paper that are laid out in a loose grid with their edges overlapping. It's offbeat, but so subtle that you can really

Preceding spreads: After P/Kaufmann bought the company in 2003, Clarence House brought in creative director Stephen Doyle to concoct a series of advertisements with a whimsical attitude. Page 30, clockwise from top left: Outdoor fabrics on sails include *Le Flora Danica, Vortice*, and *Coral*; umbrellas in *Nouveau Bizarre* and other Clarence House fabrics; sofa in *Le Forêt*; and *Kusama* hedge. Page 31: *Coriander*, woven by Rubelli. Page 32: *Raggiante* on the road. Page 33: Valise in *Songhai*. Opposite: A young Kazumi Yoshida in evening dress was elegantly captured by Horst P. Horst, the fashion, portrait, and interiors photographer—famous for his work for *Vogue* and other publications.

develop an affection for it. I was paid $750 for the pattern—but it was the first product of a decades-long partner-ship during which we created intricate multicolored prints unlike any others in the market.

When Robin and I met we liked each other, although we were very different. He thought I was very strange—wearing fake monkey fur, high-heeled shoes, and long hair. But I thought he was strange also, and that's why we became such good friends. He was very grand, dressed always in tweed, with a shoulder bag and a huge Cartier watch. He looked very English to me, very eccentric. I think it was an Oscar Wilde sort of thing. Later he became more reserved in his dress. But he always lived large. He'd rent a villa in Saint-Tropez and bring over his Rolls-Royce Corniche so he could drive around. He'd go to St. Barts for a month or more at a time. He'd travel to the great cities in Europe and stay at the best hotels. And we traveled together because he understood that artists and designers needed inspiration to create anything of value. Temo Callahan, Robin's long-time director of sales, started at Clarence House just before I did. We both remember sitting on Robin's nineteen-piece matched set of Louis Vuitton luggage while he checked out every room at the Plaza Athénée in Paris or Claridge's in London to make sure he was getting the best one!

Robin was a great teacher—he exposed me to so much and taught me everything there was to know about fabrics. I was untrained when I started working for him. He took me to museums, mills, suppliers, and antique textile deal-ers all over the world. And that's how I learned. I might have had a natural affinity, but experience honed my eye.

Opposite: Inspired by a book of Japanese botanical paintings, *Papiers Japonais* was Kazumi Yoshida's first design for Clarence House. Exquisite, subtle, and complex, the pattern garnered critical acclaim and commercial success—it is still unlike anything else on the market.

Clarence House: Looking Back

Robin's extravagant pursuit of the grand luxe found its ultimate expression in his modernist country house, Twin Ponds Farm, which he built in 1983, although work on the gardens continued for years. Architect Milton Klein designed the concrete-and-glass structure in the minimalist style of Paul Rudolph as a series of pavilions spanning a pond. Its multiple outbuildings included a guesthouse, tennis pavilion, and pool house. The austerity of Klein's architecture was softened by its relationship to nature. The house seems to rise from the pond, fulfilling Robin's dream, which was to see or hear water from every room. Its floor-to-ceiling windows frame views of gardens carefully designed by landscape architect Armand Benedek. These gardens were as much Robin's pride and joy as the house itself. His 21.7-acre property featured a Japanese garden, a rose garden, an English garden, a double allée of sixty Kwanzan cherry trees, a meditation garden, a Zen garden, and a "primeval forest" carefully designed to look wild, although Robin brought trees from all over the world to plant there. For the interiors, he hired designer Jay Spectre and his associate Geoffrey Bradfield to help realize his grand vision of modern luxury, setting his extraordinary collection of furnishings and art against a backdrop of rare wood veneers, which further mitigated the harshness of the minimalist exterior—all adding up to pure chic.

Jay Spectre had also designed Robin's New York apartment, with its green-velvet-walled living room–cum–screening room. So it was no surprise that when Clarence House moved to New York's Decoration & Design

Opposite and proceeding spread: Designed in 2000, the popular *Flowering Quince* pattern looks at home in many different kinds of interiors, despite its modernity. It can give traditional architecture a new life or bring decorative excitement to a contemporary setting. Neither fully pictorial nor completely abstract, blending Eastern and Western influences, it offers a broad appeal while maintaining a distinctive point of view.

Building in 1985, he was also engaged to design that space. With extravagance unheard of now, we occupied three floors—and the basement. The showroom featured a grand interior staircase, granite walls, and travertine and marble floors. All the furniture was reupholstered seasonally to showcase the collections—velvet in winter and linen in summer. The luxurious private dining room had upholstered mohair walls plus table linens and china that we had also designed. This showroom epitomized its era in all its opulence. It was the 1980s in full effect. It was just a few years ago that we consolidated our space in the D&D building—signs of the times.

Robin died in 2003, having sold to P/Kaufmann, the company we worked with to create more accessible textiles with our design sensibility. I miss our creative collaborations, but the team at Clarence House has continued Robin's legacy of excellence. We still have the famous shopping bag emblazoned with our multicolored logo that *New York* magazine called one of the most stylish in the city. It's still a status symbol among designers who carry the bag out of our showrooms filled with fabric samples. I continue to listen to my inspirations and produce textiles that reflect a point of view unlike any other in the market. We're a bit more practical, perhaps, but I haven't strayed from our idiosyncratic roots in the quest to produce the most exciting, exuberant fabric designs around.

Opposite: Robin designed the Clarence House shopping bag, which has become iconic—and not just among interior designers. Its exuberant brand of chic mirrors the company's daring attitude toward design. We're not afraid of risk; it offers great rewards. Proceeding spread: Kazumi Yoshida, in full color.

The Artist at Work

Before I came to Clarence House, the company's primary focus was on importing European fabrics, most of which were reproduced from antique textiles, which we call documents. There's no question that the firm had nailed the concept of luxury. But it had very few original designs. When I got there, old-world opulence was still the order of the day, but we entered a new era. The studio took off—and we became known for original designs that were like nothing else on the market.

When I started at Clarence House, I didn't know anything about fabrics. I had just gotten to New York via London, where I'd stopped for a few months after leaving my home in Japan. I was enjoying myself, going out at night, going to classes occasionally. Plus, I worked a bit as a DJ. And in the afternoons I'd work on interior renderings for the designer David Barrett or fashion illustrations for Mary McFadden.

I had studied traditional brush painting at school in Japan but didn't have much formal training. Still, Robin saw something in me—a hand, an eye, perhaps. My whole career has evolved from the collaboration that we built. Robin taught me how to design fabric. He provided me with a world of inspiration, and he gave me the best education in textiles I could ever have had. I learned on the job.

Even though I've spent the last thirty years at Clarence House developing my personal style, it's not a singular vision. I draw from many different places, other times, and varied traditions to create textiles that are relevant now. I might look to nature or eighteenth-century designs, modernist painters, Pompeiian murals, contemporary fashion, or Japanese theater. It doesn't really matter. That's because everything's filtered through the same lens— my point of view. Our collections speak to all the stylistic variety that characterizes design today, without worrying about fads or trends. We try to lead the way, not follow along.

We're trying to give decorators textiles to suit many tastes, projects, and budgets, from modest to unlimited. Robin always offered the most opulent silk velvets alongside simple cotton canvas. We do the same today, because there's never going to be one fabric that's right for every application. A beach cottage demands something

Clarence House fabrics merge art and craft. Beginning with one of Kazumi Yoshida's exuberant paintings, the joy of creation is tangible from the very start, in both color and line. It's that quality of delight that must be translated into the final textile, without losing any of the initial artwork's energy or vibrancy through the process.

The Artist at Work

different from what a town house requires. A curtain can be made from the finest sheer, but you shouldn't use delicate voile to upholster a sofa. I love the contrasting textures and sophisticated patterns of our signature cut velvets. I'm drawn to prints with eccentric, large-scale designs and intense, clear-hued palettes in a rainbow of many colors. Often, my Japanese sensibility tempers the European traditions we're steeped in. Certainly, my fascination with contemporary arts plays a huge role in the designs that appeal to me most.

Robin always gave me the freedom I needed to create. He'd rarely contradict me, even when he was pretty sure I was headed down the wrong path. When something didn't go well, he'd just say, "Kazumi, I was going to tell you, darling, but you make mistakes sometimes." But liberty and confidence take you only so far. I was lucky that he also provided the inspiration and education I needed to imagine fabrics and make them a success. And that's why our trips together became so important. Much of our travel was visiting with mills and printers, collaborating with them on production. But it was also a search for archival document textiles and rare books. Everything comes from somewhere. The source material that sparks creation makes all the difference.

Robin and I visited textile archives throughout Europe. Some were held at the mills, some were in private collections, some at museums. But French mills such as Tassinari & Chatel (now owned by Lelièvre) and Bucol (which Hermès purchased) were often the richest resources. Both are located in the city of Lyon, which has a long history of silk weaving. These firms' archives include antique textiles collected from around the world and original fabrics woven on their looms for several centuries; they have the source materials and the know-how to help us reinvent them. Patrick Lelièvre has always been one of our most supportive collaborators. He put all of his resources at our disposal, allowing us to maintain and develop fantastic quality while creating new designs.

We also collected documents from dealers all over the world. Robin liked to travel in grand style, so we always had guides and drivers, especially in China and in India. Our cars were like palaces on wheels, just taking us from

Opposite: Mixing the right colors for an artwork that will provide the basis for a fabric ensures that the painting lives in its own right, but the textile's coloration will be refined later in the process, since patterns are rendered in a variety of combinations. To refine the design, Kazumi does not go back into his first drawing, but uses sheets of translucent vellum laid on top of the original artwork for making adjustments. He'll redraw a design completely, but rarely paints on top of his initial attempt.

The Artist at Work

point A to point B in search of the most extraordinary textiles we could find. In Japan, we bought rare kimono fabric and bingata, resist-dyed cloth that was being made in Okinawa as early as the fourteenth century. We bought a fantastic eighteenth-century book on Ikebana, which provided inspiration for *Ikebono*, a multicolored design that Ratti, a great Italian manufacturer, printed for us with incredible skill.

When we were visiting an archives or sitting with a dealer and we'd come across something wonderful, Robin would say to me: "This one's going to pay for our trip." We knew that we'd be able to adapt and interpret that antique textile or draw from the pages of a beautiful rare book to create a new fabric. Sometimes we'd put out a design that wasn't commercially successful, but Robin was still happy if he could consider it an artistic success. He believed it important to have these wonderfully extravagant designs that drew people into the showroom. Everyone wanted to see them, everyone was talking about what we had done. Whether they bought that design or something else when they came in ... well, at least they were there.

Coming from Japan, I found the European traditions so alien, but if you have some kind of innate sensitivity, you learn. I learned about different periods in the decorative arts, and I learned how fabrics are constructed, woven, or printed. But however knowledgeable you become, it can be equally fruitful to look at documents purely from an artist's point of view. Then you're less concerned with conventional definitions; you can really approach them simply as pattern and color. I'm never that concerned with period accuracy. I might see an almost fussy eighteenth-century brocade, which I'd never reissue as is, and take only its decorative arabesques, leaving out the foliage—or vice versa—to make a new design. I might use one element from here, another from there, and

Opposite: Kazumi's brushstrokes are purposeful yet painterly, their fluidity evidence of the speed that characterizes the movement of his hand. Proceeding spread: *Poisson-nière*, a hearty linen cut-and-uncut velvet woven at the Leclerq-Leroux mill, with a pattern of fish and other sea creatures, laid on top of Kazumi's original artwork for it.

combine them. For a chinoiserie print based on painted silks, I chose different flowers I liked from two or three documents to make a brand-new floral. Take a fourteenth-century brocatelle reimagined in the palette of a fifteenth-century African tribal costume from the Songhai empire. By some strange alchemy, this fusion becomes the source of a contemporary geometric that looks as if it owes as much to the great designers of the 1930s as anything. There are all kinds of ways to play with the source material. And sometimes I might be as true as I can to the original pattern—but reimagine it in a totally modern palette.

I approach each fabric design as though I were creating fine art. It always starts with a sketch or a painting that will be translated into a printed or woven fabric. Not all of my paintings become fabrics, but all of my fabrics started with original art. Calligraphic marks come naturally for me. I love the exuberance of freehand brushwork. But I can also finesse meticulous rendering when that's what's called for. I can do swift, minimal brushstrokes or render with attention to fine detail. Both require a delicate touch so the patterns don't become static.

Robin understood that it was impossible for me to work a nine-to-five kind of schedule. When I get in the mood, I work on my artwork very quickly for a long time. I keep my own pace. I never analyze what I'm doing while I'm painting. I go with the flow. Most of the time I have the final product in mind. But sometimes there are accidents. A painting goes in a direction I didn't expect. And that can come out even better. It's a thrill when you see something that was just in your head come to life.

I never use sketchbooks, as odd as that might seem. Wherever I travel, whatever I see, I keep in my head. Then I come back to the studio and paint. Robin used to be amazed. "How can you remember all that?" he'd ask.

Opposite: The airy studio at Clarence House's head office in New York City has become Kazumi's laboratory, where he does all of his original paintings and drawings—and where he works with his team to translate the artwork into fabric patterns. The company's library and extensive archives of vintage and antique fabrics are also kept there, inspiration close at hand. Proceeding spread, left: *Peggy* draped atop a painting; right: fabric swatches and inspiration.

The Artist at Work

I really don't know. I just remember what I like. And I know that my memory can be distorted. Sometimes the drawing becomes as much a fantasy as a memory.

What's my driving force? I'd have to say it's creativity. What's the most important element in creativity? Playfulness. That's what I don't want to lose. A child looks at the world differently from the way we do. I try to recapture that fresh perspective, that unconscious joy. I take this work seriously, but it's not that serious.

I'm inspired by travel, nature, and antique textiles. But more than anything, I love the arts. Of course I look to painters. How could I not? But my real obsession is dance and theater. Those kinds of productions seem to me the ultimate expression of collaboration. They appeal to all the senses—you've got visual excitement in the costumes and sets, music and movement. I love when it comes together. There's nothing more inspiring to me than a Pina Bausch or Robert Wilson production.

Robin and I got to know Robert Wilson on the Concorde. Typically grand, Robin had brought caviar on board, which we were sharing—Bob came by and asked if he could have a bit. He was on the way to the World's Fair in Lisbon for the premiere of his opera *White Raven*. That was the start of our friendship. You see, it wasn't all hard work. Robin used to rent a villa in St. Barts almost every year. I'd spend one or two months in a studio there, just painting. One of my favorite designs, *Colombier*, was completed there. That kind of extended stay was unusual, though. Mostly, we'd travel and then come back to New York where I would draw in my studio from memory to create something new.

I can express anything in textiles. That's the fun of it. Escapism—I can go to a fantastic beach or charming village, without reality intruding. History—I can visit Pompeii or take a stroll through the Petit Trianon, traveling across time. Nature—I can delve into some imaginary forest or look closely at the petals of an exquisite flower. I just paint whatever I want to paint. The afterthought is to make it into a textile. That's why these fabrics are unique.

Preceding spread: *Nouvelle Orléans*, a cut velvet, was inspired by a gate at Kazumi's country house in upstate New York, but it reminded Robin of ironwork in New Orleans, hence the name. Opposite: *Colombier*, a whimsical print, was born on the island of St. Barts, where Robin had rented a villa that became Kazumi's studio for more than a month at a time in the winter. Its intricate color and pattern are masterfully printed at the Ratti facilities near Lake Como in Italy's Lombardy region.

The Artist at Work

BRINGING FABRICS TO LIFE, A COLLABORATIVE PROCESS   The fabrics I design are the product of my imagination and my experience. Inspiration means nothing unless you can make something from it. Fabric is an artistic medium like any other. You have to have a certain measure of technical expertise in order to bring your ideas to fruition, as with painting, sculpture, or music.

One essential aspect of designing fabrics is understanding how to put a pattern into repeat. Even the most free and easy patterns must be repeated at consistent intervals, yard after yard. And when you see a long stretch or piece widths together, the pattern must flow and offer a pleasing balance. Getting the balance is one of the great tricks of textile design.

Robin knew that I needed to learn as much as I could about textiles and how they were made, but at the same time, he didn't want us to be limited by conventions. We'd come up with things that didn't seem possible—or at least practical—and then figure out how to get them done. Creative director Timothy Finley, who has been at Clarence House with me for thirty years, and fellow artist Yoshiteru Kawasaki work in the studio and with the manufacturers to help translate my artwork into fabrics. Their contributions and the collaborations with our manufacturing partners—the best mills and printers in the world—have always been the key to success.

We owe so many of those successes to our relationship with Ratti, the great Italian textile manufacturer, based in Como. Dr. Antonio Ratti founded the company in 1945 when he started making silk ties. Currently managed by his daughter, Donatella Ratti, it continues to value quality and artistry. That's the combination that allows the firm to understand and achieve the heights of luxury. It has worked with top fashion designers including Valentino, Yves Saint-Laurent, Chanel, Prada, Versace, and more. Even American brands like Ralph Lauren and J.Crew have turned to the company. But in the 1980s, it started working with us to manufacture fabrics for home furnishings as well as fashion. Ratti brought most of our signature prints to life. Ratti's master engravers are artists in their own right. They can produce anything I design. With tremendous technical and artistic skill, they are capable

Opposite: Studies for colorways of a nineteenth-century French document—and other designs in development, including a drawing for *Sonia* velvet, a vermicelli pattern. Proceeding spread, left: One bloom from *Le Flora Danica*, a botanical print based on antique engravings; right: *Chinoiserie Baroque*, a chinoiserie toile, redrawn with Kazumi's particular brand of whimsy, combining crazy characters, fantastic foliage, and decorative flourishes.

The Artist at Work

of creating exquisite silkscreen-printed fabrics that have as many as fifty or sixty colors. This is a monumental undertaking, because you have to isolate the elements that are meant to be printed in each color and create a separate screen for each hue. (Think about Warhol's prints. They're only a few colors each.) Each separate screen needed to be drawn individually, and there were only one or two guys in the factory who could mimic my hand. We really challenged the printers technically—and they always went above and beyond. Now technology and cost considerations have changed the way we do things to some extent. In the past ten years, there have been great advances in digital printing. If a print has more than ten colors, we'll usually produce it digitally because of cost and speed. If a design has less than ten colors, we'll still screen-print it. And we still use screen-printing for very special pieces. It has a charming quality that's almost indescribable.

When the American Society of Interior Designers gave me the International Product Design Award for *Papiers Japonais* in 1980, I acknowledged that Dr. Antonio Ratti's printing skills—and his enthusiasm—were what made it possible for me to see such an intricate design come to life. Because he was so excited to work on something truly creative, he didn't even care about the cost. He didn't even charge us for the screens. He was thrilled when he saw the designs and just wanted to do it!

Of course, we had many other partners who were also wonderful. We found the documents for *Mosaico* and *Dragon Empress* in the archives of Etro, the Italian fashion house. Gimmo Etro, the company's founder, used to buy a lot of documents from Tibet and we developed designs together all through the 1980s. (Etro's decorators' fabric line launched in 1981, the same year I got to Clarence House.) Some of those designs are still among our best sellers. Now we distribute Etro's fabrics in the U.S., and the company has its own design studio, but our relationship continues to be a close and creative one.

There's no substitute for firsthand experience when you're working with fabrics. You can get an idea from books and pictures, but you have to hold and touch fabric to understand it. Especially with the most luxurious textiles,

Opposite: Study for a new print—and the antique document on which it is based, an Indian calico. Putting the pattern into repeat by hand, not using a computer, is quicker and more creative for Kazumi. Proceeding spread: *Dragon Empress*, an exquisite textile interpreted from an eighteenth-century Indian document in the Etro archives.

The Artist at Work

the visual is just the first step. The quality of cloth—how it drapes, how it feels to the touch, the weight, the texture, the construction, how the ink sits on the ground or sinks into it—you have to experience all of those elements that make a fabric what it is. You have to live with fabric to understand it. You have to touch it to know how it's made—and how you might be able to make something of your own.

The cut-and-uncut linen velvets, which offer such textural interest, provide some insight in terms of how we work with mills to create woven fabrics. Until recently, these were all woven in the north of France at Leclercq-Leroux, a family-owned mill located on the outskirts of Lille since the mid-1800s. The Leclercq family closed the French mill, but they continue to weave this quality in the traditional way on looms they brought to their facility in the United States. Cut velvets have been in existence for centuries, originally woven by hand in silk pile. But the linen yarn was too coarse to weave by hand, so this quality was developed in the 1920s with the advent of mechanized looms. In the early 1980s, we realized that the quality of cut-and-uncut linen velvet would be perfectly suited to contemporary designs. Leclercq-Leroux has wonderful archives, which we delve into, but we can also present them with an original design. Since I understand this process well, my painting will show where to place the cut or looped elements as well as the different colors. In effect, I have to think three-dimensionally, visualizing how the design will be. And as a result, we've produced some of our most memorable fabrics—including *Le Forêt*, *Milhaud*, and *Kanji*—with this mill.

Woven fabrics are very technical. What often happens with woven fabrics is this: the mills show us what they can do technically, and we work with them to translate our designs in the appropriate material and construction. Now that I'm so familiar with what they can do, I've gotten to know the technical limits and I design accordingly, with a particular quality of material and construction in mind. We decide that a certain pattern will look good as a hefty cut-and-uncut linen velvet or an elegant silk cut velvet or an épinglé, for example—and we go from there.

Opposite: Stylized grapevines in *La Vigne*, a refined silk damask by Art Deco master Louis Süe (the frequent partner of André Mare), which Clarence House imported from Prelle. The spirals are original to the design but presage a typical Kazumi Yoshida flourish, which reappears in different, seemingly unrelated patterns.

NEW PARTNERSHIPS   When I started at Clarence House, the company was involved in a few licensing projects, which meant that my designs would be translated into goods other than home-furnishing fabric. We designed plates for Bernardaud and sheets for Cannon Mills, as well as more accessible fabrics for P/Kaufmann Inc. Since then I've been asked a few times to work on special projects, including scarves for Mikimoto, packaging for Estée Lauder, tapestries for L'Atelier Claude Declercq, and beach towels for Hermès. Estée Lauder picked up the pattern of *Paloma* for a special limited-edition bottle of its *Pleasures* perfume and a candle with the same fragrance. The charming crewel, which features doves and flowers scattered lightly across the ground, perfectly suited a light scent that evokes the sensorial experience of walking through a garden.

I've worked with L'Atelier Claude Declercq to create wonderful tapestries based on my paintings. Claude Declercq, the owner of Declercq Passementiers, started a workshop in Vietnam, where artisans weave in the tradition of the Gobelins factory, which supplied tapestries to the court of Louis XIV and his successors. It gives people in the village work. It never has been a big moneymaker, but it was his dream. The company is producing five of my designs in limited editions of eight. It's the perfect marriage of art and craft. One of my favorites is *Jembala*, which features a stylized tree of life with fanciful leaves and imaginary fruit, a majestic but whimsical lion, and other amusing creatures. After the tapestry, I decided to translate the design into a crewel fabric and a print. Each thing sustains the next.

Opposite and above: After Christine Duvigneau, studio director at Hermès, came across Kazumi's tapestries at an exhibition in 2006, she and Pierre-Alexis Dumas, Hermès's chief creative officer, bought rights to a number of paintings to use however they chose. One of these designs, called *Paysage*, opposite, was made into a beach towel, above.

Fabric Fantasy: The Illustrated Room

Drawing inspiration from the Surrealist poet and artist Jean Cocteau, as well as elegant illustrations from the 1920s and 1930s, this flight of fantasy celebrates the exuberance of creation, the power of imagination—it's a matter of having fun. My own familiar themes are brought together in a mélange of rollicking monkeys, fantastic architecture, and abstract geometric flourishes. A shirt from Comme des Garçons was the spark for the polka-dot floor. The Japanese artist Yayoi Kusama always does polka dots too, so it also makes me think of her. The set epitomizes my personal style—free association, a free hand, and a joyous palette of bright colors. The translation from a small maquette to nine-foot-high flats was physically demanding, leaving me drained but energized. Afterward, a new fabric was born—named *Beekman Place*, it offers a way to bring home this magical scene.

Proceeding spreads: Realizing a drawing at human scale, Kazumi Yoshida let himself go wild. Just as so many artists created scenery for the Ballets Russes and other companies to great effect, it would be magical to see a performance set against these lyrical paintings, made larger than life. For now, they are simply a personal expression of joy.

Fabric Fantasy: The Illustrated Room

Above: *Hoffmann*, a silk cut velvet with an ombré effect, has all the sophistication of the Wiener Werkstätte's textiles, although it is an original design. Opposite and proceeding spreads: Reminiscent of animal skin and architectural brickwork, *Hoffmann* brings a sense of luxury to a long bench—and its three little monkeys. Such opulent textiles are best suited to light upholstery and decorative pillows; *Beekman Place*, the printed fabric this set inspired.

The Eighteenth Century Revisited

It's all about style. We're not art historians. At Clarence House, we often start by using antique or vintage textiles—which we call documents—as sources of inspiration. But we don't slavishly reproduce the document. I redraw the pattern to make it our own. Even when I'm closely interpreting a traditional eighteenth-century European design, our new iteration will unintentionally reflect a hint of my Japanese sensibility. You can see it in the relative looseness of the drawing, the whisper of something exotic.

We may tweak the design or play with scale. Sometimes we almost completely reinvent the pattern—simplifying, taking just one element and repeating it to create a new design, or combining motifs from a number of different sources. Also, we almost always reinvent the color in a more contemporary vein, while respectfully maintaining the true essence of the historical piece. A lot of these fabrics are still manufactured at mills in France that have been in operation since the eighteenth century. They've got the know-how. We just bring a fresh perspective.

To photograph textiles inspired by the eighteenth century in an appropriate setting, photographer François Halard and stylist Noemi Bonazzi brought them to the photographer's house in Arles, where they could be seen in all their glory. These fabrics were by no means designed to be used in stuffy period rooms. Rather, they bring a sense of luxury and refinement to today's interiors. Proceeding spread: Rustling silk taffeta curtains pool on the floor. The divine tieback was a collaboration with Declercq Passementiers.

The Eighteenth Century Revisited

Robin was an eighteenth-century man. He liked things opulent. He never feared going over the top. And he knew that adaptations of classic European patterns would appeal to American decorators in search of the "grand luxe." That's why they came to Clarence House. Our clients have always embraced sumptuous damasks, brocades, and lampas—a feast for the hand and eye. They're designers who love beauty, and they are always looking to help their clients reach the upper echelons of taste. But we always tried to create something for them that would express the essence of the period without simply copying antique models. My goal was to create something new in the eighteenth-century manner. You have to look at the past and reinvent it. Think of Mariano Fortuny. In the nineteenth century he created new fabrics based on textiles from the eighteenth century and earlier. His work has become iconic in its own right.

The eighteenth century was a remarkably inventive period during which many beautiful textiles were produced. When I started at Clarence House, I didn't know anything about the period. I liked contemporary design—always went for something slick and geometric. Seeing the beauty of antique European documents changed my taste.

Opposite: A pure rendition of an eighteenth-century cut velvet from a Tassinari & Chatel document, *Marquise* is reinterpreted in Clarence House colors. New palettes breathe life into classic patterns, although the documentary colorway also may be offered. Proceeding spread: *Couvert de Feuilles*, a striking black-and-white cut velvet woven by Leclercq-Leroux, combines structure and organic forms in a pattern that was drawn from a stylized sixteenth-century Italian design of interlaced branches.

The Eighteenth Century Revisited

I've really come to appreciate their variety and excellence. The magnificent scale of Baroque damasks. Delicate floral silks that are amazing in a neoclassical room. Pretty cotton prints—toile de Jouy and Indiennes. Chinoiserie—with all its whimsical charms. There was such a range, how could you not find something inspiring, even something to love? Over the course of the eighteenth century, so much was cemented in to our design vocabulary that continues to appeal today.

We've never been much for fads. We try to bring out fabrics that will be timeless. When you begin with such exquisite documents, it's hard to go wrong. Where do we find them? In Europe, we look through the archives of companies like Ratti, Declercq, Prelle, Bucol, and Etro, to name a few. Over time, these companies have collected amazing source material that provides the basis for new designs. But we also go straight to the source, finding hand-painted Chinese silks in China, cotton calicoes in India, kimonos in Japan.

We adapted our *Madeleine* floral from an eighteenth-century Chinese hand-painted silk that was originally made for export to the West. Everyone went mad for it: celebrities including Kirk Douglas, Diana Ross, Gregory Peck, and Marisa Berenson all took that one home. And Barbra Streisand used it in her apartment on Central Park West.

Opposite: Once one of Clarence House's most sought after designs, *Madeleine* is a delicate and exuberant floral. Proceeding spread: Warp-printed silks include (from left) *Feuilles de Chêne*, adapted from a Tassinari & Chatel brocade originally woven for Marie-Antoinette's private summer room; *Versailles*, a pattern from Prelle, adapted from a brocade in Marie-Antoinette's bedroom; and *Langeais*, made by Lelièvre exclusively for Clarence House from a document in the Quenin archives. *Rayure Eugénie*, a lavender-and-green silk damask, is an eighteenth-century design from the Quenin archives that Clarence House adapted in both color and pattern.

The Eighteenth Century Revisited

Warp prints, with their ethereal charm, are some of my favorites from this period. Because the fabric is woven after the warp is printed, the patterns become slightly distorted. (If you print on a completed cloth, you don't get this effect.) The designs look almost blurry and seem to vibrate, which I find exciting. Even florals created using this method have a life and energy that is unlike anything else. Movement is built into the pattern. This technique seems very well suited to fashion—the textiles would make fantastic rustling silk ball gowns. They're magnificent as curtains, fresh and sophisticated at the same time.

When you're starting with a document, you can try to re-create the exact colors. But I've had even more fun developing new colorways for large-scale woven lampas, including designs like *Josephine*, *Verlaine*, and *Nouveau Bizarre*. With a damask, you generally have no more than two different colors—one in the warp threads, which are stretched lengthwise on the loom, and one in the weft threads, which are woven back and forth, over and under the warp. To weave a lampas, you have two warps and at least two wefts. You're able to introduce many more colors because the weft threads can be fed in at intervals rather than running continuously back and forth. We use so many colors in these wild rainbows that you can't help but be enthralled. It's totally unlike anything that would have been done at the time. It's the perfect blend of then and now. To use a cliché: tradition with a twist.

Preceding spread, left: The subtle trellis of oak leaves and acorns, *Feuilles de Chêne*, has the blurry outlines that characterize a warp-printed silk, as does the multicolored floral silk, shown at right, from Tassinari & Chatel. Still printed in France, these fabrics are incredibly extravagant—and very fine. Opposite: *Cluny*, a rich silk-and-linen brocade with a striéd ground, has a traditionally opulent look and feel. The twisted metallic weft yarn gives the design its depth. Proceeding spread: A *lit à la polonaise* draped with *Verlaine*, a multicolored lampas beautifully complemented by the mattress and cushions covered in Clarence House stripes.

The Eighteenth Century Revisited

You might think of the eighteenth century as this very stuffy period in design. (The interiors look so formal to us now—and the social hierarchy was so much more rigid.) But it's not true. There was wildly inventive stuff being done. The short Nouveau Bizarre era—just five years around 1700—produced some of my favorite designs. They're so intricate; the more you look, the more you see. With fanciful flowers and animals like dragons woven into the cloth, they're not sweet at all. They're complex and asymmetrical and totally eccentric. If you didn't know otherwise, you might almost think they were some kind of contemporary riff on traditional motifs. The flowers look like they're from a Dr. Seuss drawing. But, these original designs may actually be a bit far-out for a contemporary audience! The lampas we call *Nouveau Bizarre* was an adaptation of an eighteenth-century pattern. I gave it my own sense of fluidity and a new coloration that completed its success.

Talk about whimsy. That's why chinoiserie has had such lasting appeal. After the East India Company opened up trade with the Orient in the seventeenth century, Europeans became obsessed with China—at least with their imagined vision of it. Designed to appeal to the European market, chinoiserie blended Asian motifs and Western fantasy. The theme lent itself to fanciful flights of imagination, which were translated into intricate decorative patterns. Chinoiserie was especially well suited for adaptation to the rococo style, which was also playful and expressive.

Preceding spread: The rainbow effect of the silk *Elio Satin Stripe* is decidedly modern, although it is woven using traditional methods. The highest-quality silk satin woven today, it is complicated to produce, since the loom must be warped with all the different colors. Opposite: The *Elsa* satin stripe was inspired by a Schiaparelli dress, but the scale and coloration were changed to suit home furnishings. Beautiful as curtains or upholstery, this fabric has a striking presence. Proceeding spread: The intricate new design *Nouveau Bizarre* is a modern adaptation of a document from the late seventeenth or early eighteenth century.

The Eighteenth Century Revisited

Now, when we create a chinoiserie print, we take it in ever more whimsical and wacky directions than the original designs, which can be somewhat problematic for a modern audience. I love the individual motifs you can pull out—especially the fretwork. And, I love the scenics—all the little characters in their imagined world. It's so amusing to render—like creating a set for an opera or ballet or a storybook. You get to make up all the little characters in their costumes, riding in carriages, going about their business, lounging around in pagodas and other follies. It's all about creating a lively chaos—and then taming it. It's such a puzzle to get the balance right, the rhythm and repeat. But it's very satisfying when you do. To me, the best designs have a brave scale—and a richly varied palette. That's why I think I've had success with such patterns as *La Vie Chinoise*, *Les Fêtes d'Orient*, and *Grand Tableau Chinois*. The last is based on an eighteenth-century painted-silk panel. Meanwhile, a design like *Diaghilev* captures the spirit of the eighteenth-century patterns in its extravagant follies, but it's completely concocted from my imagination. Its sharp colors are silkscreen-printed. It's destined to be a Clarence House signature.

Many designers may use similar documents as their jumping-off points, so there's some sameness in what's available. After all, classic patterns never fail to find an audience. Beautiful traditional prints were the first building block of Clarence House's business—and they continue to delight our customers. But you have to do something to make them your own. That's the kind of creativity our customers expect. And that's what keeps us alive.

Opposite: Hand-printed in Italy at the Ratti facilities, *Grand Tableau Chinois* is a large-scale design of great intricacy and whimsy. The scenes and characters were adapted from an eighteenth-century Chinese hand-painted silk. This is the kind of design in which you keep discovering new things. Proceeding spread: The vivid colors in *Les Fêtes d'Orient* add to its excitement and intrigue. It's clearly the product of a lively imagination—to wit, unexpected *coquillage*, fantastic animals, and fronds growing out of parasols.

The Natural World

There's a certain poetry in the natural world. It's not unexpected to find yourself enthralled by a plump iris, a peony so blowsy it seems about to burst, a gigantic palm frond, or a delicate herbal sprig. It's not difficult to create something charming from them.

In almost every textile tradition that influences us, botanical imagery has been reimagined in two dimensions, whether patterns are printed on cloth or woven into it. In seventeenth- and eighteenth-century Indian palampores, intricate tree-of-life designs were painted on cotton calico, the panels used as bed hangings or covers. Almost no contemporary collection comes out without at least a nod to this motif, which has become a staple in any fabric designer's repertoire, popular now as then.

Floral chintz—printed glazed cotton—was an early favorite at Clarence House. Among the brands that Robin Roberts began importing and distributing was Colefax and Fowler, the British company that was built on 1930s adaptations of eighteenth-century prints. When Clarence House cemented its reputation, chintz was all the rage.

Opposite: In rendering the vagaries of the lively, intriguing world he sees around him—not to mention the fantastical worlds that come from his imagination—intricate details are as much a part of Kazumi's art as his speediest brushstrokes. From the tip of his brush or the stroke of his pen, flowers spring to life, animals frolic, and delight pours forth.

The Natural World

But masters of each period in the decorative arts captured the botanical world in their own ways. In the late nineteenth century, William Morris based the Arts & Crafts movement on certain tenets—one of which was the relationship between people and nature. The stylized botanicals on his printed fabrics are still top-notch. A graphic tree-of-life pattern by the Austrian designer Dagobert Peche has the modern assurance that was characteristic of designs from the early twentieth-century Wiener Werskstätte movement, in which he played a part. The French Fauvist painter Raoul Dufy designed thousands of fabrics in the early twentieth century, encouraged by couturier Paul Poiret, who used Dufy's work in his fashionable coats and dresses. The painter's extraordinary Art Deco patterns were so different from anything that came before them—and actually much more graphic than his paintings. Flowers, foliage, birds, and other beasts—even elephants—were his inspiration. For much of the time he was working, Dufy was employed as a fabric designer for Bianchini-Férier, a Lyonnais silk manufacturer.

Opposite: It requires the expertise of Ratti, the finest textile printer in the world, to produce *Les Pivoines*, an intricate and vivid pattern in which skillful rendering doesn't dilute the designer's signature energy, but contributes to it. Proceeding spreads: *Bimini* offers a multicolored yet airy pattern of coral and *coquillage*; a row of garden chairs covered in a variety of Kazumi's delicately drawn prints. From left, *L'Herbier de Colette*, *Las Palmas*, *Cartouche Chinois*, *Bimini*, *La Vie Chinoise*, and *Les Pivoines*.

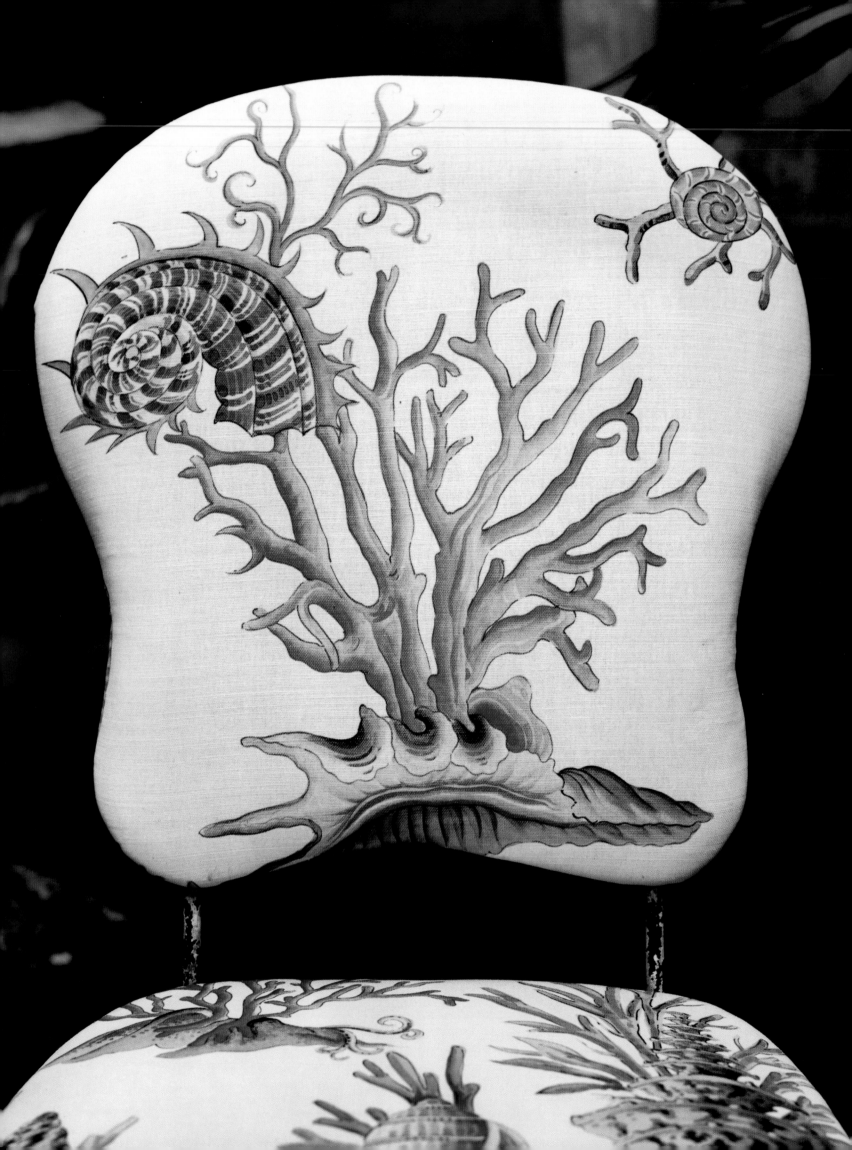

The Natural World

I try to draw from their example and make botanicals my own. I might draw directly from nature, but I can also let myself look through the lens of designers who came before me. I don't think it diminishes any kind of poetic sensibility if I'm looking to a Raoul Dufy pattern or to nature itself.

Time spent in the garden presents a wealth of inspiration—being in the sun, looking up at the sky, feeling the breeze. But I can find as much inspiration on Fifth Avenue as in the garden. *Tropicanica*, one of Clarence House's most successful prints, was inspired by a window display at the Bergdorf Goodman department store, not by any kind of stroll in the country. Walking down the street in New York one day, I was stopped by an installation of tropical leaves in varying shapes and sizes pinned to the wall, casting shadows on it. I was struck by the size of the leaves' flat planes, the variation from one to the next, and the depth created by light and shadow. Tropicals are something that have had a long appeal in decoration, but I knew I'd be able to make something different with this design.

Opposite: *Tabu*, a witty hybrid, combines trompe l'oeil ribbons patterned with leopard spots, a songbird perched on a flowering branch, and a little chinoiserie scene. It packs a lot into one design. Proceeding spread: *Tropicanica*, a striking botanical design, was drawn in a way to create a dramatic dimensionality.

The Natural World

I got back to the studio and painted the design from my memory. Ratti ended up hand-printing the fabric that came from this painting using twenty separate screens. *Tropicanica* is a complicated pattern—exquisitely drawn with an attention to fine detail you don't see much in fabric design today.

Papiers Japonais, the first printed fabric I ever designed for Clarence House, encapsulates the balance that I look for in my work. It's a kind of "less is more" botanical. I found myself fascinated by a book of botanical drawings found in a museum in Tokyo. So different from Western versions, the drawings were linear ink sketches with just a hint of color. They were so delicate; I really liked them. So I started to sketch flowers from a Western botanical book in a Japanese way, leaving them a bit unfinished, with just a hint of color, a suggestion of blossoms and leaves. Then we scattered the sketches on the floor. The way they lay on top of each other created shadows so interesting that I made them part of the overall pattern. That collected collage of drawings became the final artwork for the printed fabric. The design is so offbeat, but it's subtle. Your affection for it can develop over time. Lee Radziwill used this print. She used it on the walls in her New York penthouse apartment. *Botanica* presents another riff on the same idea. It also has the trompe l'oeil effect of sheets of paper, but it is somewhat less delicate.

Opposite: The enduring appeal of *Papiers Japonais* stems from its unusual delicacy and complexity. The lyrical interplay of pencil sketches, light washes of color, and attention paid to certain leaves and blossoms gives it an unfinished and captivating quality. At once modern and timeless, it offers an Asian sensibility, the perfection of imperfection.

The Natural World

Of course, nature is not just plants, trees, and vegetation. Perhaps even more fascinating than the botanical world is the astounding richness and whimsy of the animal kingdom.

Where does it start? With monkeys, of course. I've always loved the trickster. So, too, have other artists—Rousseau, Picasso, and even Léger. The French painter Marie Laurencin designed a hand-block-printed wallpaper for André Groult called *Les Singes* sometime before 1920.

Sometimes my zoology's painted with precision—other times with abandon. *Le Palmyre* is very traditional in its rendition, for example. But in *Congo*, zebras dance and play across an impressionistic landscape, the energy of freehand brushstrokes reflecting their leap. *Jembala*? A majestic lion, stylized monkeys, and sassy lizards frolic in the multicolored leaves and tendrils of a stylized tree of life; this one has become a Clarence House signature. I adapted the design from one of my tapestries and now we've got both crewel and printed versions. *Polly* is a romp of birds, striped, polka-dotted, patterned beyond what nature might allow—almost Aztec in their air.

Above all, I try to keep things inventive and amusing. It's the imaginative rush that keeps you on top of your game.

Opposite: *Giacometti Zoo* was inspired by the ironwork in furniture by Diego Giacometti, the influential modern sculptor and designer. Note the energy that derives from the strength of the diagonal lines, the whimsy of the figures, and the depth that comes from using slim dark shadows to give the trees and animals a sense of three-dimensionality.

The Natural World

Above: Woven by Rubelli, heavyweight *Galeazzo* has the look of needlework. Its host of stylized animals includes lions, tigers, gazelles, and even rabbits. Opposite and proceeding spread: *Tibet*, an original design in cut-and-loop linen velvet, was inspired by a Tibetan rug. With the traditional lion-dog motif redrawn, placed in repeat, and recolored to graphic effect, it offers a bold exoticism.

Fabric Fantasy: The Clothes Horse

I like the idea that my fabrics can take on a life of their own. They only reach their full potential when someone else takes notice and turns them into something wonderful. The collaborative process starts as soon as a drawing leaves my studio—and it really never ends.

Because they are meant for decoration, it might seem that bringing these fabrics to life is a simple matter—sewing up some curtains, upholstering a chair. But to me, it's more than that. When my fabrics are used, they become party to a life well lived. They join a shared artistic vision. And that's exciting.

When the photographer François Halard and stylist Noemi Bonazzi decided to take my fabrics to the south of France to photograph them, I knew it would be a round robin of inspiration. They used them to dress up a herd of small white Camargue horses, an ancient breed that once lived wild near Arles. It's a charming idea—and sort of silly. But that's the crux of it. We all need a little fantasy. We should all be inspired to play in creative ways.

Using fabrics like these, it's easy to design interiors that feel like a fantasy. Tent a room, upholster the walls, envelop yourself in pattern and color. Take your imagination to the limits—and create rooms of arresting beauty.

Proceeding spreads: A Camargue horse with his blanket made from *Diaghilev*, a multicolored fantasia of follies (both classical and orientalist), coral, and palm trees. This recent design is screen-printed at Ratti; *Royal Palm* embroidery in neutral tones; *La Magique d'Orient*, another flight of fancy blending chinoiserie and abstracted modern flourishes.

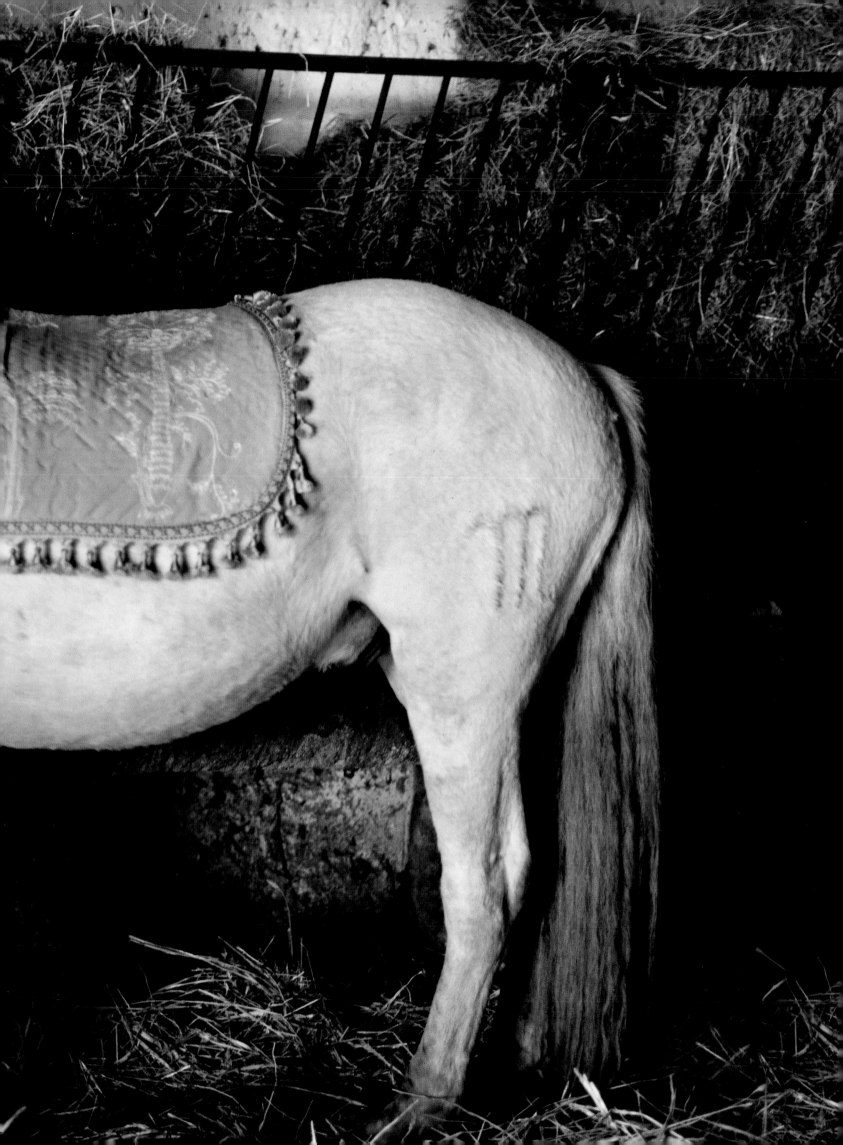

Modernist Abstraction

Although Clarence House's early success was built on importing fabrics based on eighteenth- and nineteenth-century documents, modernity quickly made its way into the firm's core lexicon. Robin's interests evolved and he found himself turning from Marie-Antoinette to Napoleon III to the masters of Art Deco. I had always been inclined to modern design, so it made sense to me.

Fabric patterns that pay homage to the important movements in twentieth-century art and design became a signature for the firm in the 1980s—as they are today. Our greatest influences in this evolution were early Modernism—including the Bauhaus and Wiener Werkstätte in design and Fauvism, Cubism, and Futurism in fine art—and Art Deco. Named after the seminal 1925 Paris exhibition (the Exposition Internationale des Arts Décoratifs et Industriels Modernes), Art Deco was in many ways the culmination of these earlier movements, all of which influenced its development throughout the nineteen-thirties and forties. During this period, the look of interiors changed. While avant-garde, they were also luxurious and refined, and the fabrics of the time followed suit.

The syncopated rhythms and edgy geometry of patterns inspired by art and design from the early part of the twentieth century appeal to a taste for the avant-garde, which came to Clarence House over the course of time. However, the rarefied sense of luxury that characterized many Art Deco interiors was always a part of this firm's DNA. Many of the fabrics in this section have African antecedents; early Modernist artists and designers frequently incorporated imagery and objects from African art into their work.

Modernist Abstraction

In typically grand manner, Robin sometimes stated his primary hobby as collecting masterpieces of twentieth-century decorative arts. He constantly searched out paintings and furniture that would convey his obsession with the beauty and luxury of inventive design. Even his Aston Martin expressed that passion. He had informed and discriminating taste—he was the very definition of a connoisseur.

Robin lived with furniture by Émile-Jacques Ruhlmann, Louis Süe and André Mare, Pierre Chareau, Albert Cheuret, Diego Giacometti, and Armand-Albert Rateau. He also had many pieces by Karl Springer and Jay Spectre, although their work was of later vintage. The combination of rational geometric forms and opulent materials appealed to him and to me. And like modernists before him, his collections included fine African and pre-Columbian masks and ceramics. We both loved the way Jean-Michel Frank blended Art Deco style with African artifacts and modern art in projects like the famous Rockefeller apartment. That kind of heady blend really is the ultimate.

Opposite: *Harlequin Quilt*, a weighty wool patchwork inspired by African fabric. Proceeding spreads: *Kinshasa*, a cut-and-loop linen velvet with geometric designs inspired by an African textile juxtaposed with a tribal mask; *Armand*, a silk cut velvet drawn from Robin Roberts's Rateau chair; *Botswana*, a printed linen with a stylized giraffe pattern.

Modernist Abstraction

Of course, I was highly influenced by my exposure to Robin's penchant for collecting. To experience what it was like to live with such pieces through his eyes opened mine to great design. At the beginning, I was really just a kind of club kid. I was interested only in what was happening "right now" in music, in art, in fashion, in theater. And I still find it so engaging and important to keep up on everything. But now I can look back, too. I have more perspective. And that started with Robin's influence.

I don't subscribe to one school at all. My interests range widely. I consider myself a creative interpreter as much as anything. But if there's one artistic movement whose influence on my geometric abstractions comes through most strongly, I guess I'd have to say it would be Cubism. I love the syncopated geometries of Picasso, Braque, and Fernand Léger. And I've been inspired by the painter Sonia Delaunay, who created similar patterns in softer palettes about the same time. (Delaunay also designed many fabrics that had echoes of her painting style.)

Opposite: *Ellington*, a cut-and-loop linen velvet woven on looms brought from Leclercq-Leroux's French mill to the firm's U.S. facility. Note the difference in tones between the cut and uncut sections; even though the same hue of thread is used, they read differently because of the technique. The geometric forms recall the shifting rhythms of jazz.

Modernist Abstraction

My *Arboles* pattern was drawn from a Picasso painting—its subject was a woman lying down in the landscape. I liked the shape of one of his trees, so I isolated that element and repeated it. Turning it this way and that, I created a new pattern that we rendered in cut velvet. Rhythms such as these suit our weighty cut velvets. But vivid patterns also translate well into strong and sprightly prints that can be colorfully exuberant or architecturally rational or both at the same time.

Of course, most art historians feel the course of Cubism would have been different if Picasso hadn't become fascinated with African tribal art. Just take a look at *Les Demoiselles d'Avignon*. I've also been continually fascinated by African patterns, whether I'm looking directly at textiles from Mali or Yoruban cloth—or if I'm nodding to Modernist paintings and sculpture that drew inspiration from those other cultures. You can look here and there—anywhere really—and create something that reflects your point of view, your interests, your own particular passions.

Opposite: Inspired by 1920s designs, *Poiret* is a heavyweight épinglé weave, meant to look like needlepoint. Figures, foliage, and a few funny mushrooms rendered in a bold palette contribute to its amusing air. Proceeding spread, left: *Cristobal* and *Patout*, two simply elegant cut velvets based on 1920s documents, woven at the Quenin mill. Right: *Arboles*, a complex geometric cut velvet, riffs on one element—a tree—from a Picasso painting.

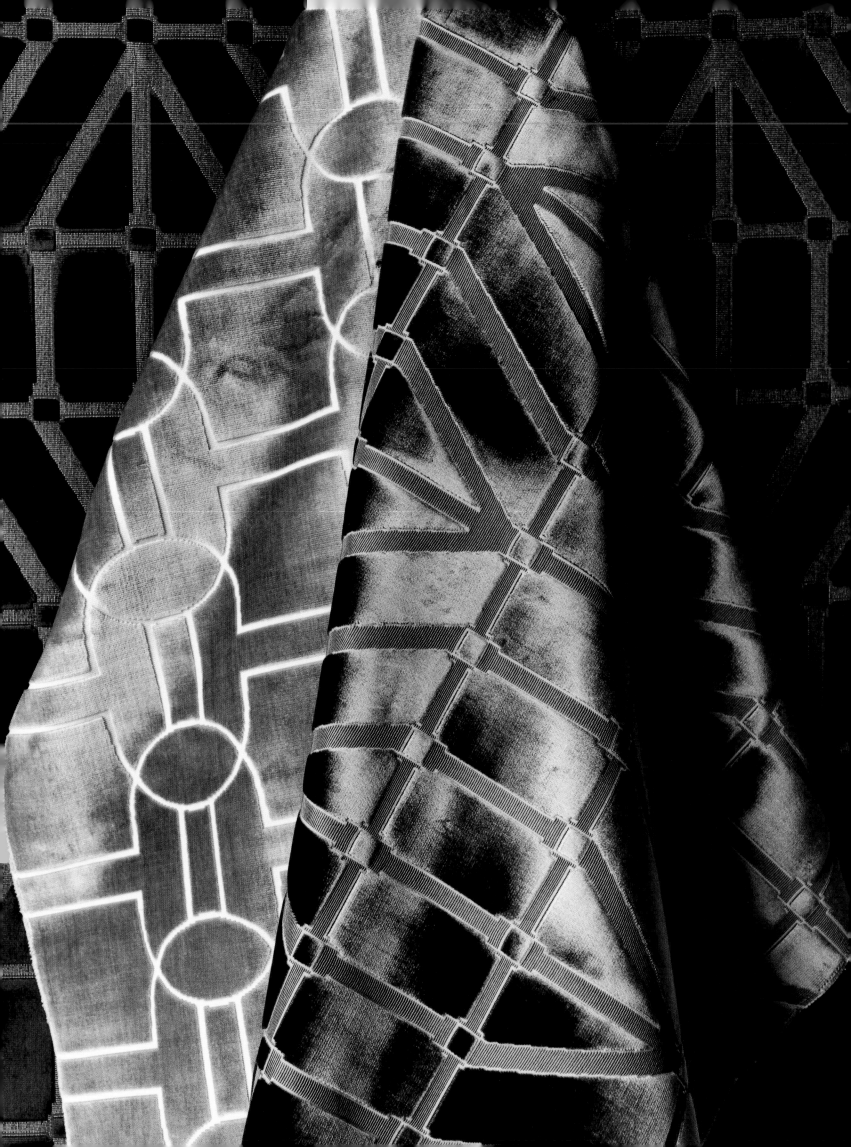

Modernist Abstraction

Some of the geometric patterns that feel the most modern are based on classical designs. That's why a labyrinth pattern rendered in silk cut velvet feels equally appropriate (and decadent) cladding barrel-backed Ruhlmann armchairs or a classical bergère. But it also works for pillows on a Billy Baldwin tuxedo sofa.

When I'm designing fabrics, I always look at fashion, theater, and visual arts—it's fascinating to me when those disciplines are intermingled. I think that's a big part of the reason I'm so intrigued with the Ballets Russes and the Ballets Suédois, two early twentieth-century companies whose productions stretched the definition of ballet beyond its classical traditions. The patterns and colors of the sets and costumes from those productions—particularly the Orientalist fantasies—inspire me, as they have designers such as Paul Poiret and Yves Saint-Laurent, both of whom were almost as intrigued with interiors as they were with fashion.

What's more, both of these innovative ballet companies enjoyed collaborations with avant-garde costume and set designers, and hired great artists to create sets and costumes for them. Pablo Picasso, Georges Braque, and

Preceding spread, left: Derived from a striped ikat document, *Operato* is a striking reinterpretation of the original design in a double-layered silk-and-cotton pocket weave; right: The gradations of tone in *Léger* are especially impressive because the pattern is screen-printed by hand at Ratti. Opposite and proceeding spread: The characters in *Zambezi*, a cut-and-loop linen velvet, were inspired by costume designs for the Ballets Suédois.

Modernist Abstraction

Fernand Léger all worked with Sergei Diaghilev, the impresario who dreamed up the Ballets Russes. And Léger went on to design many productions for the Ballets Suédois as well.

Lately, I've been very much influenced by Léger. The way he combined a gradation of tones within overlapping geometric shapes influenced certain of my fabrics and one tapestry. The cut-linen velvet we call *Zambezi* features monkeys and birds drawn from Léger's costumes for *La Création du Monde*, performed by the Ballets Suédois. I look at images of Léger's drawings for the production and think: Wouldn't they make great fabric?

Even now, I'm just as inspired by going to see Pina Bausch's company perform or going to a museum to look at paintings by Van Gogh, Bonnard, and Vuillard as I am by anything, really.

On the practical level, sometimes geometric patterns are just what you need in a room. I live with them more than I do any other kind of pattern. Geometrics have existed in almost every culture, at every time, from stone-work on Mayan temples to Chinese characters. And now they have become an essential part of the Western design sensibility. They can come from almost anywhere. But they always work. Architectural and rational, they make sense in so many places. They can be a little challenging. But they are meant to appeal. And so they do.

Opposite: The fluid line in *Velours Moderne* cotton velvet shows Kazumi's hand—and a measure of restraint. Proceeding spreads: Juxtaposed with African art, *Mozambique* combines a stripe inspired by mudcloth and that evergreen, a leopard pattern; *Masai Deco*, a textural geometric design rendered in sumptuous cut velvet—and its sculptural counterpoint; *Diana*, a subtle animal-patterned jacquard; *Bouclé Zèbre*, dramatic in black and white.

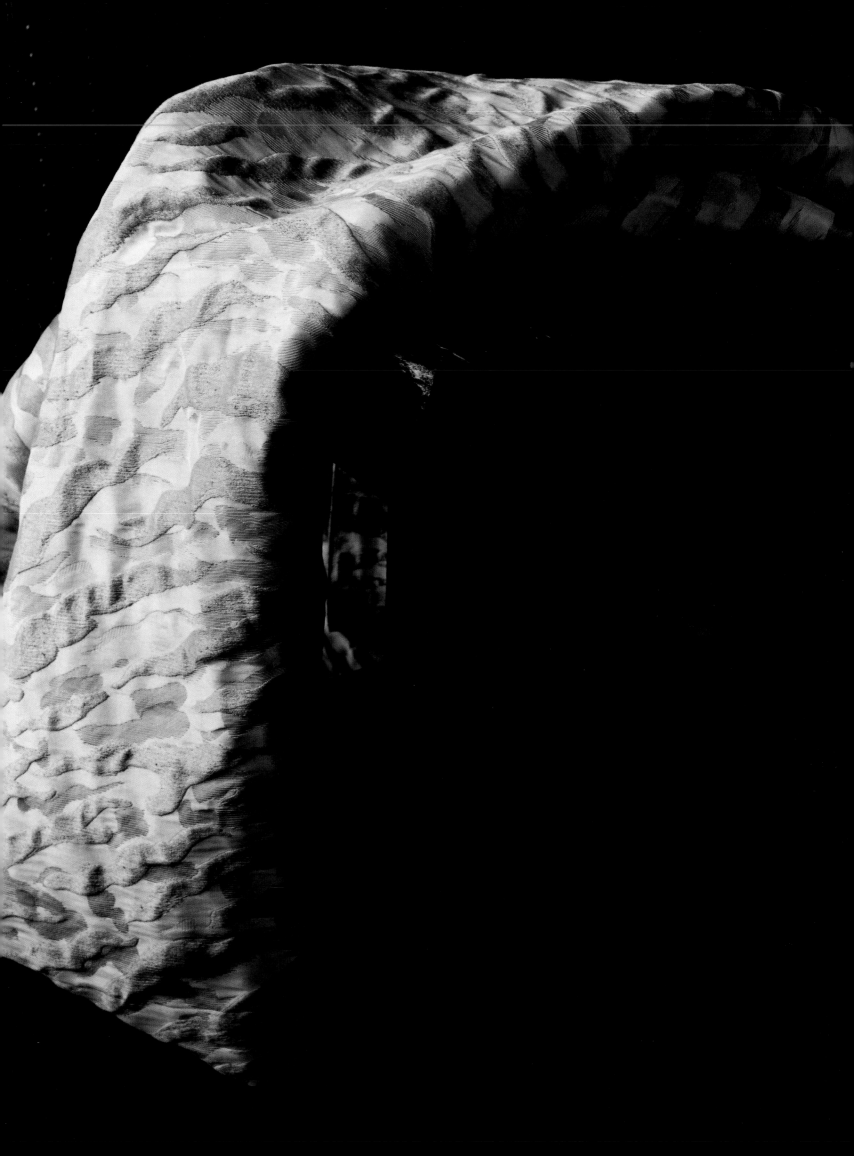

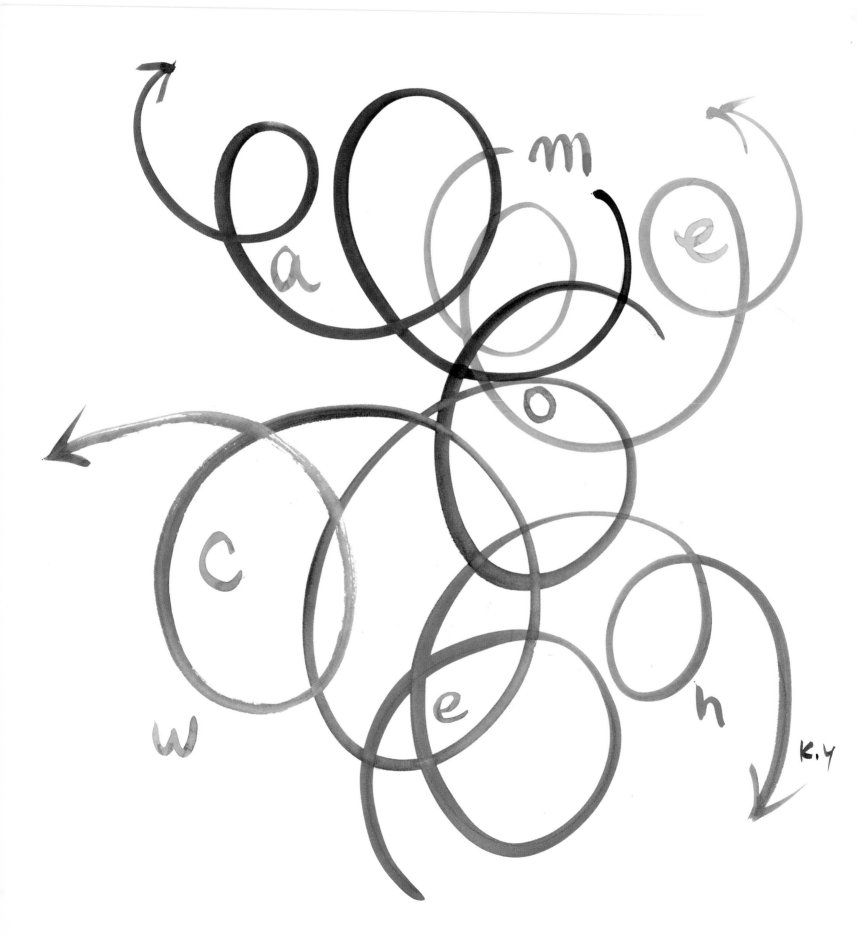

Freehand Prints

Contemporary printed fabrics with a painterly aspect have become one of Clarence House's strongest signatures. And that's because these designs are in some ways the most "mine" of anything we do. They all start with an original drawing or painting. And even though there's a whole process that goes into producing the printed textiles, you get the impression that the patterns are painted directly onto the cloth. It's still amazing to me how closely the final product matches my initial artwork—and that's what's exciting: the immediacy.

These dynamic prints are the sum total of my early training and my years of experience. My fluid, gestural style started when I was a young boy at school in Japan. Practicing the calligraphic gesture is part of the training when you learn Japanese ink drawing. But it came naturally to me. With the confidence I've gained over the course of time, I've felt my work getting looser and looser, which is the goal. I want it to flow easily—and almost unconsciously. To me, it's clear that a sense of movement is one of the most important aspects of a successful fabric design. That's what keeps the patterns from becoming static when they're put to use in a room. That's what keeps

When Kazumi lets his mind wander—and his paintbrush—he can head off in many different directions. But the thread remains—his singular hand. Robin often said Kazumi had the best hand for fabric design he had ever seen, a statement rarely disputed. And at Clarence House, the artist has been given free rein to the greatest extent possible.

Freehand Prints

me engaged as I'm painting. And in the end, that's what gives these designs their sense of joyfulness. I'm happy when I'm painting them. And I think that comes through. That's why people have always responded well to them. Because the patterns make them smile.

What's it all about? Freedom—giving the artist's hand free rein. When I'm holding the brush, it swoops and dips across the page almost without my guiding it. After so many years, it's instinctual. I'm tapping into visual memories collected over time—and letting them flow out through my paintbrush.

To me, these prints are special. They're eccentric and varied because the subject matter can be anything that comes to me. Because they come as they will, depending on my whim, they're never really much like anything you'll find from another fabric designer—and they're very personal. I'm inspired by the world around me—fashion, travel, design, or simply walking down the streets of New York.

I love patterns that are pure abstraction. *Vortice*, a personal favorite, is swirls upon swirls. It looks like I let myself go. And that's what happened. But I also love the funny faces in a pattern like *Jules et Jim*, which was inspired by classical sculpture. And I can't get enough of the vivid colors in *African Masque*, a quirky take on something collectors take quite seriously. You have to have fun sometimes—if not all the time. How else to keep it fresh?

Opposite: The curly-headed youths in *Jules et Jim* are based on classical statues, but their sense of whimsy transcends the source material. Proceeding spread: *Vortice*, in the original black on a white cotton-linen ground and in red on an acrylic fabric for outdoor use. The pattern has been so popular that it was also printed in metallic on a linen ground.

Freehand Prints

You can certainly see the influence of the Fauves in this aspect of my work. I love the painterly gestures and bold palettes that artists such as Henri Matisse and Raoul Dufy brought to their paintings. This French movement is undoubtedly one of my favorites. The Fauves' brushstrokes aren't consciously something I try to emulate, but the link is undeniable.

Matisse was a fabric lover, for sure. In photographs of his studio, you can see African Kuba cloths and Tahitian bark cloth on the walls. But he also collected textiles from Europe, Turkey, and North Africa. He lived with them and they played a part in his paintings, as backdrops and abstracted patterns.

Raoul Dufy actually supported himself as a fabric designer and as a fine artist. His Art Deco patterns were game-changing—amusing, creative, often even genius. He became one of the most influential fabric designers of the twentieth century, thanks to the modern, large-scale patterns that he created for the couturier Paul Poiret and Bianchini-Férier, the Lyonnais silk manufacturer.

Other twentieth-century artists created textiles based on their drawings. Painter Roger Fry opened the Omega Workshops in England in 1913. Fellow painters Vanessa Bell and Duncan Grant, who were also in the Bloomsbury

Opposite: *Zucca*, a contemporary print adapted from the Ratti archives with the original blotter, a paper copy of the printed design, which is created to make sure the screens are correct. Proceeding spread: Printed in this summery colorway of blues and browns and in an exciting multicolored version, *Mougins* is an imaginary landscape named for the medieval French village near Cannes, a mecca for artists and celebrities where Picasso spent the last years of his life.

Freehand Prints

Group with him, joined Fry in blurring the boundaries between fine and decorative arts. The Omega Workshops employed artists to create a host of household items, intending to bring new excitement and a sense of spontaneity to interiors. They created textiles, unfettered by ideas of what fabric should be or what people wanted to live with. Their patterns were loose and painterly, but at the same time geometric. These are the kinds of designers who moved the world of textiles forward, as they did fashion, art, and so much more.

Anouk is one of my recent fabrics that got a lot of critical acclaim. For this design, I was inspired by Sonia Delaunay, but rendered her kind of geometry in my own more painterly hand. A brushy stroke mitigates the structured pattern. The bright colors recall her palette. The magazine *Harpers & Queen* took up the fabric and created a fabulous photo spread with a model in a coat made from the pattern, but it didn't stop there. They also covered a car in it, which the model stood in front of. And they took a very exciting picture—it was the epitome of chic.

Opposite: *Anouk*, one of Kazumi's original designs, is printed on a linen ground, which gives the bright palette a gutsy base. Even in the blocks of color, there is a sense of his brushstrokes. Proceeding spread: *Fernand*, another of the artist's original abstractions, offers extraordinary depth, vitality, and gradation, echoes of Cubism.

Freehand Prints

While each design is certainly my own expression, when someone chooses to bring one of my fabrics home, it's also a reflection of an attitude toward decoration. These fabrics appeal to people who bravely believe decoration should be fun. When you use them in a room, their striking patterns can become the star, so why not take the plunge? Bold prints clearly complement modern interiors. In a pristine space, they can really sing a lively tune. But they also bring contemporary flair to a room with more traditional style. They make beautiful curtains—you can just imagine swaths of pattern flowing at the windows. They're not for the timid—they bring so much life to a room.

Opposite: Fabric framed as artwork. Above: *Jungle Book*, a youthful appliqué inspired by an African textile. Proceeding spreads: Clockwise from top left against black wall, prints include *Congo* in blues, *Anouk*, *African Masque* in brown, *Kinta*, with characters drawn from the Ballets Suédois, *Vortice*, *African Masque* in red, *Jembala*, and *Primavera*, a modern paisley; against brick wall from left, *Congo*, *Jules et Jim*, *Congo* in blues, and *Kinta*.

At Home: Living with Fabric

When I come home to my apartment in New York, I'm not particularly interested in delving into the past. But neither do I want to live in a pristine white box. I've made a life in the decorative arts—and I like having art and decoration surround me. It's modern luxury I'm after. That's about filling your life with texture, comfort, and beauty.

Because my apartment's in downtown Manhattan, just on the edge of SoHo, it feels appropriate to live with modern and sophisticated designs. I collect art and I live with my own work. As for the rest, I like to keep it simple. Neutral walls—white or gray. Clean-lined furniture. A few pops of color that come from the artwork and modern tapestries on the walls or the floor. Eighteenth-century patterns and Louis XV furniture don't work for me here. It's fine to make your home into some kind of fantasy if you want to be transported. But that's not really my style.

In his New York City apartment, Kazumi surrounds himself with color and pattern through contemporary art and modern furniture, and his own work and that of other artists he admires. A serene atmosphere prevails, but his natural curiosity allows him to continually assess the environment he has created—and constantly evolve.

At Home: Living with Fabric

My furniture is mostly Modernist—Wiener Werkstätte, Art Deco, mid-century. I also have some avant-garde contemporary pieces. I don't pretend to be a decorator. I just find something I like—and then I find the space for it. And I like to move things around when something new comes into the picture. It comes together somehow.

I choose what I will bring home carefully and with a measure of restraint, focusing on the beauty of each individual piece. The overall harmony of a place is important to me—but as an artist it is less important than gathering around me objects and material that I find myself drawn to for whatever reason. I do that without wondering whether or not they fit into some kind of unifying vision. The unifying vision is my own sense of aesthetics, which comes naturally at this point. A strong sense of geometry sometimes draws me in—or a considered gesture. The reason I fall in love is usually that I see a specific point of view that somehow intrigues me. It's pretty intuitive.

Opposite: The entrance hall contains a wide-ranging mélange—a table by the French industrial designer Roger Tallon; a contemporary chair by Satyendra Pakhalé, an Indian designer based in Amsterdam; and one of Kazumi's oil paintings. Proceeding spread, left: *Art Moderne*, an abstract print; right: Kazumi's living room with Art Deco seating expansive enough to hold a number of pillows, a Declercq tapestry on the floor, and his sculpture above the fireplace.

At Home: Living with Fabric

In the country, the fabrics I choose are a bit more eclectic—a floral or two might even creep in. But at home in the city, I tend toward bold geometric designs. They suit the linearity of my furniture. My cut velvet *Labyrinth* looks great on the slatted Josef Hoffmann chair. A black-and-white zebra-patterned velvet is graphic enough to bring a feminine silver Art Deco bergère up to date. I keep the boxier Deco pieces—my sofa and club chairs—in solid mohair, throwing a mix of patterned pillows on top. The variety in their textures is so alluring. When you sit on the sofa you can't keep your hands off them.

The thing about using geometric patterns is that you can mix them—almost at will—without running into too much trouble. In the guest room, a large daybed is covered in two contrasting patterns. Both combine linear and organic motifs. On one, circles are placed at regular intervals inside stripes. The other's an undulating squiggle, also tamed inside a stripe. I guess that explains why they work together. Animal patterns also work well with geometrics. There's an intriguing tension between free-form shapes and a regular rhythm, which never fails to please the eye.

Opposite: In the entrance hall, *Labyrinth* silk velvet suits the geometry of a Josef Hoffmann chair, so modern in its simplicity. Just a cushion is sometimes enough when it comes to such luxurious fabrics. Proceeding spreads: A close look at *Minos* cut velvet highlights its texture; left, *Zebra* silk velvet; right: A generously sized daybed is clad in complementary fabrics—*Velours Moderne* on the mattress and *Velours Dia* on the frame and bolsters.

At Home: Living with Fabric

Geometrics feel modern in a way that echoes the architecture of this apartment. A clean envelope with some contemporary detailing, it's not quite a blank slate. Rather, it allows me to mix together what I love most.

The textiles that I embrace at home without restraint are my tapestries. The Claude Declercq Workshop makes these pieces in a Vietnamese factory that Claude started in 1996. The techniques are traditional, but the results are not. Each tapestry can take more than a thousand hours to weave. To me they are like having paintings in the house. They're the closest thing to art in a textile. They're not in repeat. They're each one big panel. I love that they hang on the walls or are on the floor as rugs. They have such strength and character. Each one defines its own space. You really can't layer them. You want each one to stand on its own. Each one needs room to breathe. I really love living with them. I love taking note of the differences between the way an image looks as a painting and as a woven piece. I love the unexpectedness of having such a strong pattern on the floor. And, more strong pattern on the walls. In contrast, it's best to keep the upholstery quiet but strong, simple enough to stand up to the pattern, complement it, but not compete with it. Not everyone could live like this. But I like to have my things around me.

Preceding spread, left: *Les Pois*, an original design based on a pattern in an Ottoman costume with Marc Newson's Felt Chair; right, a mid-century-inspired print on a wool ground, meant to look like an épinglé weave. Opposite: Kazumi's tapestry *African Masque*. Proceeding spread, left: *Kanji*, a graphic cut-and-loop velvet; right: the bedroom with a pillow in *Zambezi* and accordion-folded panels with Kazumi's mother's calligraphy.

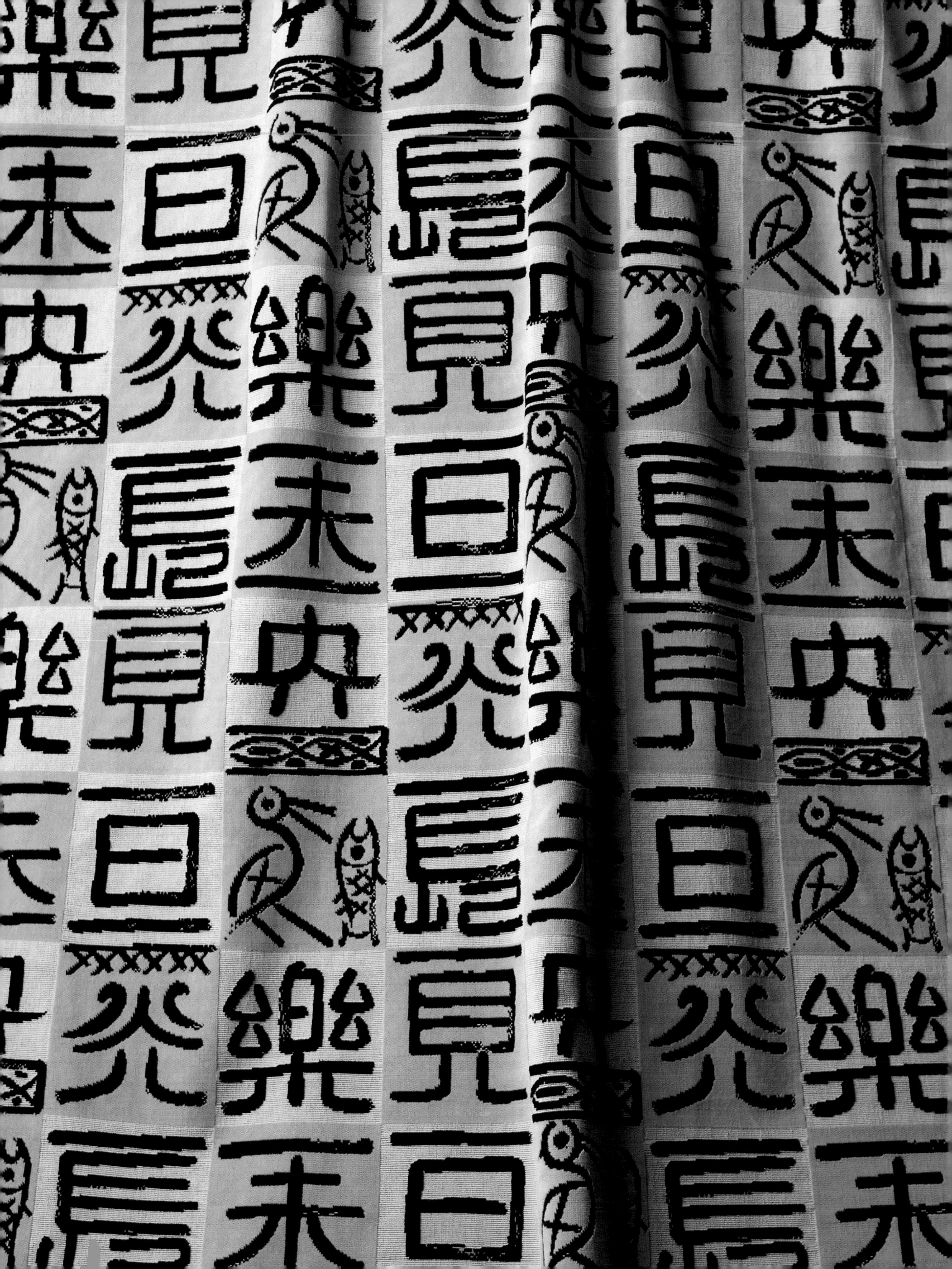

Glossary

BOUCLÉ Fabric woven using a bouclé yarn, which is made from threads that are looped and twisted together. Textural and hard-wearing, bouclé may recall the look and feel of a classic Chanel suit.

BROCADE A rich textile traditionally woven with gold or silver threads in a raised pattern that may appear embroidered. Popular in the eighteenth century for fashion as well as home furnishings, it is still prized for its look of opulence and considered quite formal, although frequently woven without metallic threads.

BROCATELLE A three-dimensional fabric with patterns in high relief. Often a blend of silk and linen, it is commonly woven with two warps, creating raised designs in satin against a twill ground. Sometimes described as having a blistered or puffed appearance, as seen on the proceeding spread in the *Songhai* pattern, a graphic silk and linen blend.

CHINOISERIE Fanciful European interpretations of Chinese motifs in European decorative arts, popular starting in the seventeenth century. Chinoiserie reached its peak in the mid-eighteenth century, blending particularly well with rococo styles, and has been a recurring theme in textiles, furniture, artwork, and architectural structures, especially follies.

CHINTZ Painted or printed Indian cotton, imported to Europe starting in the early seventeenth century for use in dresses and household textiles, and eventually copied in Europe, England, and America. Today, the term refers to glazed cotton fabric, often printed with floral designs. Revived in the 1930s by designer John Fowler, chintz had another heyday in the 1980s among decorators aspiring to the English country house look, and these florals continually cycle back into fashion, beloved for their old-fashioned charm.

CREWEL Embroidery, typically rendered with a variety of stitches in thick wool thread on a linen or cotton ground for a textural, multicolored effect. Intricate Jacobean designs with flowing vines and leaves are traditional, but Clarence House uses traditional techniques to create modern designs, as seen opposite in the *Amazonia* pattern.

DAMASK Sumptuous woven textiles that originated in China and arrived in Europe via Damascus, a hub of the silk route—hence the name. Traditionally woven in one or two colors of silk using one warp and one weft yarn, the pattern is defined by the contrasting sheen of figure and ground; the fabric is reversible, depending on whether one wants the figure or ground to be glossier. Typical designs include stylized florals in symmetrical arrangements.

DOCUMENT Industry term for antique or vintage textile used as inspiration for a new fabric design.

DOCUMENTARY PRINT Printed fabric that is a reproduction of a historic printed textile.

ÉPINGLÉ Essentially an uncut velvet with looped pile.

GAUFFERED, GOFFERED Embossed surface finish achieved by pressing fabric between heated rollers. Usually a finish used on velvet, also linen.

IKAT Fabric woven with a resist-dyed warp or weft, resulting in a pattern with a blurred effect. It is an ancient technique found throughout Asia, Africa, and Central and South America. The name is derived from the Malaysian word *mengikat*, meaning to tie or bind. In recent years, ikats have seen resurgence in popularity.

Glossary

INDIENNES Cotton prints imported to France by the French East India Company starting in the seventeenth century—and the imitations produced later in Europe. Unpretentious, even when intricate.

JACQUARD Textile produced with a mechanical Jacquard loom, which uses a punch-card system to automate weaving. Joseph-Marie Jacquard invented the loom in 1800 in France; it can be used to create elaborately patterned tapestry weaves, brocade, damask, brocatelle, and more.

LAMPAS An intricate fabric similar to damask, created using two warps and many wefts in order to weave a muticolored pattern in relief.

PASSEMENTERIE Decorative trim—including braid, gimp, tassels, beads, and fringe, as seen on proceeding spread.

PRINT Fabric with designs achieved with colorant, in essence ink or dye, applied to fabric by any number of methods, including the following:

>   Block printing: Form of hand printing in which the design is carved onto wood, linoleum, or metal blocks. One block is used for each color. The dye is applied to the face of the block and then the block is pressed or hammered onto the fabric. A very old technique.

>   Digital printing: Designs are applied to fabric using an inkjet printer. A recent development.

>   Silkscreen printing: Printing method by which the pattern is blocked out on a mesh fabric stretched on a frame—the screen—so when color is squeezed through, it will penetrate only the unblocked areas. Each color in the pattern requires a different screen.

RESIST DYEING A tinting process in which wax, clay, or knots protect areas of material from the dye.

SATIN Lustrous, tightly woven fabric with a glossy surface and dull back, often silk. Pure glamour.

VELVET Fabric with a short, soft, cut pile. It can be created by weaving two cloths face to face with interchanging pile ends that are cut on the loom to produce two separate pieces of velvet. In an alternate method, the pile ends are looped, then cut by wires inserted widthwise, like the weft. Velvet can be made from cotton, mohair, linen, or silk; the material helps determine the properties of the textile. Silk velvet is the most refined and luxurious. Linen has a dry, almost rustic hand. Mohair velvet is plush and dry.

>   Cut velvet: Fabric with a pattern that consists of velvet figures (cut loops) raised against a background formed by uncut loops, as seen opposite. The cut pile is higher than the uncut pile.

WARP Threads that are set lengthwise on a loom forming the structural basis for the warp threads to run across.

WARP PRINT Printed textile with warp threads that are printed prior to weaving the fabric, which gives the design an indistinct outline and subdues its colors. Derived from the word for variegated, *chiné* is the French term for the technique, used in Lyon's silk industry since the eighteenth century to create floral fabrics prized by Marie-Antoinette's court.

WEFT Threads running from side to side on a loom, generally carrying the pattern.

Acknowledgments

Kazumi Yoshida thanks the Kaufmann family for providing a home that fosters creativity, Dorothy and Harry Lawenda, Patrick Lelièvre, André Leclercq and his family (Leclercq-Leroux), Philippe Verzier and Guillaume Verzier (Prelle et Cie), the Rubelli family, Bucol, Antonio Ratti and family, Jacopo Etro and the Etro family, Claude Declercq, Jérôme Declercq, Koji Yano, Stephen Doyle, Harold Koda and Alan Kornberg, Temo Callahan, Pat Sadowsky, Maurice Bernstein, Fabio Bellotti and Daniela Morera, Charles Miers, Philip Reeser, Sabine Rothman, Sam Shahid, Betty Eng, and finally his partner, James McGovern, for his endless support.
Special thanks to the creative team in the studio: Timothy Finley, Yoshiteru Kawasaki, and Joann Breznicky.

François Halard thanks Anne-Sylvie and Mathieu Bameule, Nicole Echalier, Victor Picon, Chris Gosney, and the Small Darkroom.

Noemi Bonazzi thanks the following people and businesses who were invaluable in the making of this book: Alex Brannian, John Gauld, Readyset, Pascale Ouattara at L'Atelier du Midi, Lightbox Studios, David and Kelly Martinez at Stitch, Paula Rubenstein, Mia Ferrari Liebmann, Esme Viedermann, and Claire Buchanan.

First published in the United States of America in 2011

Rizzoli International Publications, Inc.,

300 Park Avenue South, New York, NY 10010

www.rizzoliusa.com

© 2011 Kazumi Yoshida   Photography © 2011 François Halard

Editors: Philip Reeser and Sandy Gilbert Freidus   Production: Colin Hough-Trapp

DESIGN BY SAM SHAHID

2011 2012 2013 2014 / 10 9 8 7 6 5 4 3 2 1

Distributed in the U.S. trade by Random House, New York

ISBN-13: 978-0-8478-3566-9

Library of Congress Catalog Control Number: 2011926685

Printed in China